D1461645

ST. PATRICK

His Writings and Muirchu's Life

History from the Sources

ST. PATRICK
His Writings and Muirchu's Life

edited and translated by
A. B. E. HOOD

History from the Sources
General Editor: John Morris

PHILLIMORE

1978

Published by
PHILLIMORE & CO. LTD.,
London and Chichester

Head Office: Shopwyke Hall,
Chichester, Sussex, England

©

Text and translation: A. B. E. Hood, 1978
History from the Sources series: Mrs. Susan Morris, 1978

ISBN 0 85033 299 0 (case)
ISBN 0 85033 300 8 (limp)

Printed in Great Britain by
UNWIN BROTHERS LIMITED
at The Gresham Press, Old Woking, Surrey

CONTENTS

ACKNOWLEDGMENTS

DR. JOHN MORRIS died of cancer on 1 June 1977; he is sadly missed by his many friends and colleagues.

This book now appears in the shape which he had envisaged. Before his death he had supervised the production of the texts and translations and had drafted his historical introduction; but he had intended to provide fuller annotation and discussion of some of the Patrician problems. In the circumstances it has seemed best to the publishers and myself to print that introduction as it stood, with the minimum of necessary additions and alterations.

It was John Morris who first introduced me, with his customary enthusiasm, to St. Patrick and who then guided me so patiently in producing this volume in the *History from the Sources* series. My thanks are due above all to him; also to Professor O. Skutsch for help and advice.

It will be obvious from the preface that any work on Patrick and the associated Latin texts must be indebted to Professor Ludwig Bieler's publications; certainly these present texts and translations depend gratefully on his scholarship.

A.B.E.H.

SIGNS AND ABBREVIATIONS
USED IN TEXT AND NOTES

*	textual note
†	textual corruption
[ ]	word(s) interpolated in manuscript(s), and to be deleted
⟨ ⟩	word(s) omitted from manuscript(s), and to be inserted
om.	omitted by
del.	deleted by

For abbreviations used to indicate manuscripts (A=Book of Armagh, etc.) see Preface.

INTRODUCTION

Patrick was the effective founder of the Christian Church in Ireland. He was consecrated bishop and came to Ireland in 432. He stayed in Ireland until his death, about 30 years later, and was the first Christian to make any substantial number of converts, and to leave behind him a lasting organised church.

His life and work are exceptionally well recorded.[1] Two of his own writings are preserved; they are the only documents that have survived from the British Isles in the century after the fall of Rome; and a biography, composed by a Leinster priest named Muirchu about 200 years later, drew upon lost contemporary texts. These documents are here reproduced, in the original Latin, with an English translation.

But in spite of unusually full and clear evidence, the story of Patrick has suffered feverish distortion at the hands of interested ecclesiastics, from the later seventh century onwards. He founded and organised a church, with many converts, including several persons of royal and princely origin in north eastern Ireland. But though converts were many, they were still a small minority, and Christianity did not in his time become the national faith of the Irish. In the words of the modern scholar most deeply acquainted with the literature of early Christian Ireland, Patrick 'was not entirely forgotten, but such evidence as we have regarding the two hundred years following his death seems to show that his memory had slipped into the background of old and far-off things.'[2]

The traditions of Ireland and Britain emphasise that in southern and central Ireland the Christian church was founded independently of Patrick, a generation after his time, and also long remained a minority faith. The mass of the Irish population was not converted until the expansion of the monastic reform, in the middle decades of the sixth century. A hundred years thereafter, the Irish church was torn by controversy between those who sought conformity with Rome and Europe in organisation and in external symbols and those who clung to traditional ways. Controversy was fierce for more than two generations, and in its later stages the adherents of conformity with Rome revived and magnified the name of Patrick, the true founder of the Irish Church, who had been canonically ordained and had conformed with Rome. The zealous interest preserved his own writings and Muirchu's biography, but it also submerged his memory in a flood of added fiction.

The only valid evidence for Patrick's life is contained in his own writings, in Muirchu's biography, and in the external records that explain the circumstances of his appointment. He himself describes

1

his background and youth. He was a Roman Briton. His father was a *decurion*, a town councillor and local magnate, and also a Christian deacon; his grandfather, and perhaps also his great-grandfather, had been a Christian priest. His father owned a substantial estate, maintained by a large number of servile cultivators, probably in southwestern Britain. At the age of 16 he was taken prisoner by Irish raiders, and served as a slave herdsman for six years, probably in north-eastern Ireland, until he escaped. He travelled 200 miles to find a ship, and after three days' voyage landed in a deserted countryside, which he and the ships' crew traversed for 28 days before they came to human habitation. The long voyage suggests a landfall in Gaul rather than in Britain, and the extensive uninhabited land suggests Brittany. The ship that carried him in his clandestine escape was evidently no ordinary merchant, but was manned by emigrants or refugees, for the captain and crew abandoned it on making land, and Patrick says nothing of storm or shipwreck.

Patrick also says nothing of the next few years, save that at some time he acquired friends in Gaul; but Muirchu reports that he spent a long time at Auxerre; and one fragment, perhaps from Patrick's pen, also reports a visit to 'the islands of the Tyrrhene sea'[3] as well as to Italy. These were chief centres of the reform movement that was reshaping western Christianity in Patrick's youth. Until the end of the 4th century, Christianity had been almost entirely a religion of the towns, so much so that the Latin word for countryman, *paganus*, became the ordinary word for heathen or non-Christian; and the great majority of bishops were urbane, well-to-do gentlemen, with little sympathy for the rustic boor, and no interest at all in the baptism of barbarians beyond the frontier.

Established views were challenged and shaken by Martin of Tours, a generation before Patrick's time. He was the first hermit in Europe. In the east, holy ascetics of the desert were older than Christianity, and in the early 4th century Christian ascetics flocked to the deserts of Egypt and the Near East in large numbers. They were termed *monachi*, monks (from the Greek word *monos*, lone) because each sought to live alone by himself in direct communion with God; but they were so numerous that they were compelled to live in large communities, the first Christian monasteries. In the west, a few wealthy individuals took a personal monastic vow, and lived retired ascetic lives on their own estates with a few companions. From the later 4th century, some reforming bishops encouraged their diocesan clergy to take personal monastic vows, and housed them in monasteries attached to their cathedrals.

Martin quickly earned widespread fame and honour as the only solitary ascetic of Europe, and against his will was chosen bishop of Tours in 372. He refused to live in the bishop's town house, and established himself in a cave two miles from the city, where he established a monastery and a school for 80 monks. He offended his fellow bishops because he was 'shabby and ill dressed'[4] and no gentleman; and he was also the first to preach systematically to country people in his diocese. His two best known pupils were Victricius, who became bishop of Rouen, and is the first Latin Christian known to have made converts and founded monasteries among barbarians beyond the frontiers, in the territory that is now Belgium, and Amator, who became bishop of Auxerre, and there founded a cathedral monastery.

Martin died in 397. Just before his death, Victricius visited Britain, and won decisive majority support for Martin's reforms in a synod of British bishops; probable immediate consequences of his visit included the foundation of monasteries at St. Albans and at Whithorn in Galloway, among the barbarians, and of a church of Martin at Canterbury. But Martin's initiative was not widely followed in Europe. Reform took a new direction after 410, when the capture of Rome by the Goths shocked many men into new thinking. A young nobleman named Honoratus founded a new kind of monastery on an island in the Tyrrhene Sea, Lérins, off the coast that is now known as the French Riviera. It was a high-powered seminary whose aim was to train dedicated and scholarly monastic clergy, and to persuade the cities of Gaul to choose them as bishops. Lérins succeeded, and among its most eminent monks were Hilary, who became bishop of Arles, the chief city of southern Gaul, and a young Briton named Faustus, who came to Lérins while Patrick was in Gaul, succeeded Hilary as abbot, and in time became bishop of Riez, in Provence; his extensive writings are the foundation of future Gallic theology. On the mainland the most forceful ally of Lérins from its early years was Germanus, a close friend of Hilary, who succeeded Amator at Auxerre in 418.

This was the Gaul in which Patrick won friends. The isolated statement attributed to him, that he visited Italy and the Tyrrhene islands, evidently Rome and Lérins, is quite possibly true. But they were not the most important places in his early life. Muirchu says that he set out for Rome, and on his way spent a long time with Germanus at Auxerre; he does not say whether or not the journey to Rome was ever completed. By Muirchu's time, tradition already made his sojourn at Auxerre last for 30 or 40 years, but one detail that Muirchu misunderstood gives à more exact indication of the time. He says that Germanus had Patrick consecrated bishop by Amator, an 'important bishop who lived nearby';[5] he had previously implied that Germanus consecrated him. He evidently used a source that mentioned consecration by bishop Amator, but did not state his see. Since Amator was Germanus' predecessor and died in 418, its meaning was plainly that he ordained Patrick as priest or deacon; evidently as deacon, since Patrick was hardly as old as 30, the minimum age for a priest, by 418.

Patrick was at Auxerre before 418, and finally left the city in 431 or 432. But his stay was not continuous. He himself says that the voice which commanded him in a dream to escape told him that he was to return to his homeland, and after his account of travel by sea and through deserted lands he continues 'again a few years later I was in Britain with my kinsfolk.'[6] It was evidently his first return after his captivity, for his kinsmen welcomed him and begged him never to leave home again after his tribulations. The 'few years' since he left Ireland had been spent abroad, at Auxerre, perhaps also at Rome and Lérins. But Patrick was resolved. In another dream he was visited by 'a man named Victoricus'[7] who urged him to return to Ireland and convert the heathen. The man was evidently Victricius of Rouen; Victricius is the only European ecclesiastic known to have urged or practised missions to the heathen and to have had an important following in Britain in the time of Patrick's father.

But Patrick could not go on his own. Muirchu reports that after the vision he left home and came to Germanus at Auxerre, who ultimately secured his appointment to Ireland. The appointment was entirely novel, for Victricius had on his own initiative preached to barbarians on the borders of his own diocese, but neither the Pope nor the bishops of Gaul had yet consecrated any bishop to any heathens beyond the frontiers of Rome. The decision was a by-product of more urgent ecclesiastical politics. One of the sequels to the shock of the fall of Rome in 410 had been the triumph of the views of the great African bishop, Augustine of Hippo, who rooted a disciplined, centralised church upon the doctrine that all men are from birth condemned by the sin of Adam, and may be saved only by the Grace of God, in practice bestowed by a sacrament, administered by a canonically ordained priest. Augustine's principal opponent was a British scholar long resident in Rome, Pelagius, acknowledged by his enemies as the most polished Latinist and most learned theologian of the day; until 410, Pelagius' old fashioned liberal views remained orthodox, but by 418 Augustine had triumphed, and Pelagians were condemned as heretics by rescripts issued by the imperial government. But in 410 the imperial government had renounced authority over Britain, and authorised the British to establish an independent government and look to their own defence. Rescripts issued in 418 were no longer valid in Britain, and the British church remained Pelagian, immune to the new doctrines of Augustine.

By the late 420s, British Pelagianism seemed a menace to the bishops of Gaul and to the Pope. In 429 'on the initiative of Deacon Palladius Pope Celestine sent bishop Germanus of Auxerre as his representative to confound the heretics and guide the British to the Catholic faith.'[8] The Chronicler Prosper, who reports the event, was a friend of Palladius, who was the Pope's personal deacon and possible successor. Germanus' biographer, who was also a well informed contemporary, a friend of Germanus' companion in Britain, reports the visit in detail and makes it sound as successful as he can; but though he claims widespread popular support for the visiting bishops, he is unable to cite any significant achievement of its aim; no synod condemned the heresy, or was even convened to hear the Pope's emissary, and no ecclesiastic is reported to have been deprived or to have changed his views, though Germanus' visit is said to have been approved by a convention of Gallic bishops.

When Germanus' visit brought no result, Rome took more drastic action. Prosper reports that in 431 Palladius came to the British Isles in person, with a stronger status than a papal envoy; the Pope consecrated him as 'first bishop to the Irish Christians'.[9] The exceptional appointment emphasises the seriousness with which Rome took the problem; no Latin Pope had previously consecrated a bishop to any barbarians anywhere outside the empire, and the despatch of the principal priest of the city of Rome to a remote island was not prompted solely by new-found missionary zeal. Prosper's summary of Celestine's struggle against the Pelagians in Italy and elsewhere stresses the stronger motive; 'in consecrating a bishop to the Irish, while striving to keep the Roman island Catholic, he also made the barbarian island Christian.'[10] The first motive was the struggle against Pelagianism in Britain; the British bishops would not listen to the Pope's emissary, and in the 430s the Pope had no power to intrude a bishop into an existing British see. In creating a new see for the Irish, he was able to introduce an important orthodox leader among the heretics. But the new bishop also had to discharge the duties of his see; though Prosper exaggerates in claiming simply that he 'made Ireland Christian', he plainly visited Ireland and made some converts.

Palladius was appointed as bishop to Irishmen who were already Christian. They may have been numerous, for many Irish colonists had been settled for more than a generation in western Britain, most numerous in Demetia, modern Pembrokeshire, with parts of the adjoining counties; many are likely to have embraced the faith of their British neighbours, and to have made some converts among their kinsmen at home, most of whom lived in southern Ireland; and Irish tradition credits Palladius with several foundations in Leinster, the nearest coast to Pembrokeshire. The wording of Prosper's summary, published about 435, implies that Palladius was then dead; and shortly afterwards his office of papal deacon was filled by Leo, afterwards Pope Leo the Great. Irish tradition held that Palladius was ill-received, and left within the year, dying on his way back to Rome.

Muirchu relates that in the meantime Germanus had made a similar proposal. Some years before, Patrick had resolved to go to Ireland, and had attached himself to Germanus; he could not achieve his ambition without powerful support from established ecclesiastical authorities. Muirchu's account complements the contemporary notices of Prosper and of Germanus' biographer. Patrick himself says that his dreams of Victoricus' urging him to visit Ireland first came to him in

Britain, but could not be realised for many years. Muirchu says that he had many such dreams while in Auxerre; and he undoubtedly pressed Germanus to support him. Germanus in the end consented, and despatched Patrick, still a priest, in the care of a senior priest, when he heard of Palladius' appointment, which provided a 'suitable opportunity'.[11] But on their way, they heard of Palladius' death, and Patrick was then consecrated bishop in his place.

Patrick himself says that his appointment was approved, against considerable opposition, by a synod of British bishops. Some objected to his personal unsuitability, since his captivity had interrupted his education before his Latin was fluent, and left him semi-literate; for, like most men of his class in Britain, he was bilingual, speaking both his native tongue and Latin, but writing only in Latin, for British was unwritten. Others objected to the mission itself, asking what was the point of risking danger among enemy heathen. His family tearfully intreated him not go, offering public inducements.

The circumstances of the day explain his need to win the approval of the British clergy and the British government, and also explain the divided views that his intention aroused. The clergy had recently survived a papal attempt to plant among them an alien who was in their view an overbearing heretic. Patrick was no theologian; his writings show no trace of Pelagianism, but also no trace of August-inianism. He was not only uninterested in theological controversy; he detested ecclesiastical politics, for they interfered with his single minded aim, his long cherished ambition to convert the Irish, whom he had come to love during his captivity. But he came to Britain as the nominee of Germanus and the successor of Palladius, heir to two continental bishops who had tried and failed to impose their authority over the British church. Patrick had to disprove the suspicion that he was a third alien intruder; his evident passionate sincerity proved that he was not to those who had met him, but it was not evident until they met him.

The despatch of a British bishop to the Irish also involved both governments.[12] The new ruler of Britain was Vortigern. He had recently enlisted a naval force of Saxons from the lower Elbe; Irish tradition reports that in the early 430s the Saxons raided the Irish coast and showed the potential strength of their fleet. Tradition also reports a treaty, sealed by a marriage alliance, between the Irish and British governments; its consequence was that Vortigern's overran and subdued the Irish colonists in western Britain without interference from Ireland. The Irish government was intimidated, and gave the British bishop grudging licence to preach without intimidation. The spread of Christianity in Ireland clearly suited the British government; but in Ireland Patrick appeared to conservative and established opinion as a hostile foreigner imposed by force, preaching the faith of the national enemy, and corrupting the youth; his was 'a strange and troublesome doctrine . . . brought over seas from far away . . . that would overthrow kingdoms . . . and destroy their gods'.[13]

Patrick struggled against enormous difficulties. He had first to convince Roman churchmen that the conversion of heathen foreigners was in itself desirable; he was suspect to his fellow clergy in Britain; and in Ireland he appeared in the guise of an enemy agent. He overcame the obstacles because his devotion defeated suspicion and his resolution prevailed against threats and hostility. Muirchu's biography pays particular attention to his first months in Ireland. He sailed up the east coast, failing to find a welcome at several ports, and eventually landed and made his headquarters at Saul, near Downpatrick, in Ulster. There he tried to visit his former master, Miliucc, but was thwarted by suspicion, for Miliucc committed suicide in fear at his approach. He then made a direct challenge to the major national religious festival at the royal centre of Tara, which coincided with the Christian Easter; his resolute confrontation of the chief druids, or *magi*, and his defiance of the High-King, earned him the nominal submission of constituted authority, and gave him continuing licence to preach unhindered.

Patrick's own account outlines the sequel in general terms. He travelled widely; he met persistent opposition from regional rulers, and was imprisoned at least twice for short periods, but suffered no greater violence. He made numerous converts, including the sons and daughters of some local kings, and also some slaves, as well as free and unfree persons of varying status in between. Often he had to pay kings to grant permission for their children, subjects and slaves to follow him; many of his converts, especially the women, took monastic vows; and he ordained several priests.

The crisis that stung Patrick into issuing his *Declaration* blew up after he had been a dozen or more years in Ireland, when he was in his late fifties. 'I was attacked by a number of my elders, who came and brought up my sins against my arduous episcopate . . . After thirty years they found a pretext . . . in a confession I had made before I was a deacon . . . I had told a close friend what I had once done as a child . . . God knows if I was fifteen years old at the time.'[14] The attack came at last 30 years after his sin as a fifteen year old, perhaps 30 years after its confession; the probable date is about the early 440s. The elders who made the attack were evidently British ecclesiastics, for the single practical decision which Patrick announces is his refusal to come to Britain; and he attaches to his refusal a warning that he could also go on to visit the brethren in Gaul. He clearly refused a request or demand. His appointment had originally been approved by a synod of British bishops; another British synod now claimed authority over the bishop of the Irish.

Patrick was again involved in ecclesiastical politics; he was bitterly distressed at the conduct of his friend, to whom he had long ago confessed his childish sin in confidence. The friend had none the less strongly supported him when he was endorsed as bishop, in 431 or 432; but had now turned against him, broken his confidence, revealed his confession, and used it impugn his fitness for his episcopate. Patrick's life's work was at stake. The reason he gave for his refusal to come to Britain was that he feared to waste the labour he had begun. He did not mean that all would be undone if he took a few weeks leave of absence, for his plea was that Christ had commanded him to be with the Irish for the rest of his life. He meant that if he admitted the authority of the British church by attending at their summons, he would be unlikely to return to Ireland, and risked replacement. But he did not trust the British bishops to win the confidence of his Irish converts. They were 'intellectual clerics',[15] products of the opulent gentlemanly society of Roman Britain, whose elegance and subtlety had offended Germanus in 429; and many of them regarded the Irish simply as enemy barbarians. They were naturally suspect to the Irish; Patrick's own rustic simplicity had broken down suspicion, but other British clergy, less sympathetic in their outlook, caused trouble. The earliest list of ecclesiastical regulations of the Irish Church, known as the *Canons of St. Patrick*, is probably in essence the work of Patrick and his clergy in the middle of the fifth century; it includes a rule that forbids British clergy to preach in Ireland without licence from the Irish church, and the rule was clearly devised in the light of experience. The Irish church had need of British clerics, and several of those named as Patrick's younger contemporaries in the late fifth century were British by name and birth; but Patrick and his colleagues needed to be able to choose those who were temperamentally suited to their task, and to reject the unfit. It may well be that Patrick's rejection of unsuitable British clergy had been the occasion of the dispute, the reason that prompted the British church to assert authority.

Patrick rejected the metropolitan claims of the British episcopate. Something of the sequel is outlined in the terse notices of the Irish Annals and in Muirchu. Under the pontificate of Leo the Great (440-461), the Annals note his 'approval' (*probatio*) of Patrick. The word is no technical canonical term, and does not concern Patrick's theology, which was never in dispute; and the surviving abbreviated transcripts of the Annals knew nothing of its context. It is a simple ordinary word, meaning no more and no less than it says. The Pope approved Patrick's episcopate in Ireland. Patrick's own *Declaration* and Pope Leo's policy elsewhere combine to give the general and particular context. The bishops of Britain witheld approval and claimed supremacy over the Irish church, and Patrick threatened to appeal over their heads to Gaul, where his old patron Germanus was now the senior bishop, in frequent contact with Rome. Leo's principal ecclesiastical endeavour was to assert the direct authority of Rome over individual sees, and to diminish the authority of provincial synods and metropolitans; the bitterest dispute of his pontificate was with Hilary of Arles, metropolitan of the Gauls, over the right of appointment to a Gallic see. When the Irish and British churches were in dispute, Leo could not do otherwise than approve the independence of the Irish church from Britain, and assert its direct dependence upon Rome. The notice of the *probatio* places it only within the 20 years of Leo's pontificate; but an additional entry may indicate a more precise date, for under the year 443 the Annals enter, without explanation, the short comment 'Patrick flourished'. It may mark the year when Leo recognised the independence of the Irish church.

Two of the embroidered tales in Muirchu have some external confirmation, and both indicate a widening of Patrick's activity after his approval. At an unspecified date he is said to have installed one of his Irish converts as bishop of the Isle of Man, with the participation of two bishops with British names.[16] The story is muddled, but its reality rests upon the two other bishops; for the consecration of a new bishop required the laying on of hands by at least three existing bishops, and Patrick could not by himself consecrate bishops. He needed the collaboration of two sympathetically minded British bishops.

The second story is of greater moment. The Annals date the foundation of Armagh to 444, the year after the likely date of Patrick's independence. Armagh is situated within short walking distance of Emain, now Navan Fort, the ancient holy centre of the Ulaid kings, who are said to have been expelled thence soon after 300, and replaced by the new dynasty of the Airgialla. Muirchu gives a detailed circumstantial account of Patrick's vigorous insistence on the Armagh site.[17] The regional Airgialla ruler, Daire, offered him a site at the foot of the hill, but Patrick demanded the hill top, which in Irish was known as Daire's Fortress; and after very considerable pressure, he obtained it, and built his church thereon.

Two items of circumstantial evidence bear upon Muirchu's story. The tradition of the Irish genealogists lists the kings of the local dynasty, and names the mid-fifth century ruler Daire; but they are wholly unaware that he was the Daire of Muirchu's story, though they meticulously note other kings who were reputed to have granted the lands upon which other major monasteries were built. Their tradition is wholly independent of the legends of Patrick and Armagh and of Muirchu's account, but it concurs in naming the same king at the same time and place.

The second item is a more recent archaeological discovery. Excavation in the churchyard of Armagh has revealed that the hill-top was in fact fortified; carbon dating of the rapid silt from its defensive ditch indicates that the fort was constructed within a few decades of 300, at about the time when Daire's ancestors are said to have deprived the Ulaid of half their territory, including their ancient centre at nearby Emain.

Muirchu describes the foundation of Armagh at length and with emphasis; but he does not assert that it became Patrick's principal centre. On the contrary, all reports agree that he remained at Down-patrick, and there died. His first and permanent headquarters were located in the lands that the Ulaid had retained, near to one of their chief royal residences. Armagh was founded at the centre of a neighbouring kingdom, a decade after Patrick had established himself among the Ulaid. But it became the seat of his acknowledged successors, and was early accorded a primacy among the later sees of Christian Ireland, its bishop named first in papal letters addressed to the Irish bishops.

In his later years, Patrick wrote his *Letter* of protest to king Coroticus; it followed an earlier lost letter, that had been delivered by a priest whom Patrick had trained since childhood, and was there-fore despatched when he had lived some 20 or 25 years in Ireland. The name Coroticus is one of the commonest, oldest and longest lived names used by the British and Welsh; it was first recorded at the time of the Roman conquest of Britain, in the first century AD, and was then spelt Caratacus by the Roman historian Tacitus; its later spellings include Ceredig, Cerdic and Caradauc, and it remains in modern use as Caradog. Muirchu names Coroticus as king of Ail (i.e. of Dumbarton, on the Clyde); and the British genealogies independently report a Clyde king of that name in the mid fifth century; Muirchu adds that he was soon after struck down by the hand of the Lord for his offence against Patrick. His ships had raided the Irish coasts, seizing prisoners whom they sold as slaves to the Picts and heathen Irish, probably Irish colonists in western Scotland. The prisoners included recently baptised converts, whom the raiders refused to return. The coasts concerned were evidently within easy reach of the Clyde; Patrick was still active in Ulster.

The several texts of the Annals give the date of Patrick's death as 17 March 459, and various texts indicate that he was between 60 and 63 when he died; the latter age is more probable, since he reached Auxerre not later than 418, and he says himself that he was about 22 at the time. He was therefore born not later than 396. His death left a vacuum that only Rome could fill, for there were no other bishops in Ireland to consecrate a successor, and the British bishops were no longer responsible for the Irish see. Appropriate measures were taken. Half a dozen northern Irish bishops are recorded in the generation after Patrick's death, each established in a separate kingdom, most of them resident within walking distance, or a short drive, of a royal centre. Few of the new bishops' seats became permanent sees, but they marked a first adaptation of Roman ecclesiastical organisation to a barbarian land. Roman practice had always established bishoprics at the centres of lay political authority; and within the Roman empire such centres had been cities. Ireland had no cities; its political centres were royal forts, and the importance and boundaries of the several kingdoms were still in a state of rapid change. The sees of the late fifth century represented only the political realities of that generation, and the regions in which Christians were numerous enough to warrant a bishop. The creation of a number of sees enabled future bishops to be consecrated at home; and whatever canonical authority they possessed necessarily rested upon the approval of the Pope, either of Leo, who died in 461, or of his successor, Hilary.

No source reports the foundation of the northern sees; only their existence is recorded, usually at the death of each bishop. The traditions of the south are, however, clear and emphatic. Four sees, each in a principal kingdom, each wholly independent of Patrick, were held to have been founded simultaneously, between 461 and 468, by Pope Hilary, who consecrated the first bishops in Rome, and was assisted by prominent ecclesiastics of western Britain, whose guidance the Irish shortly afterwards rejected. All these tales agree that Christians were then few in southern Ireland, and priests rare and hard to find. A few monasteries are also recorded, but women's houses were far more prominent than men's.

Christianity seized hold of Irish society in the decades after 530. Its impetus and model came from a reformed British church, whose novel structure was welcomed in Ireland; and was inspired by the example of St. Benedict in Italy. The civil society of Roman Britain, that had bred the genteel urban bishops whom Patrick criticised, was swept away in the second half of the fifth century, in the course of a long war against the Saxons, or English; and the aftermath of the war left a corrupt and servile episcopate, dependent upon the pleasure of warlord kings, detested by rich and poor, cleric and layman. In reaction, south-western Britain was swept by a monastic movement, that for the first time in Europe matched the scale of the original monastic upsurge in Egypt, 200 years earlier. The Irish also suffered from the uncontrolled ferocity of upstart local dynasties, and immediately adopted monasticism as enthusiastically as the British. Abbots quickly inherited the popular respect that had formerly been paid to Druids, and Irish Christianity was rooted on monasteries and identified with them. The episcopalian church of Patrick and his successors continued, governed by rules that provided for an ordinary married secular clergy, as was then normal in the Roman church. But it was overshadowed; the bishop and priest were reduced to the status of ecclesiastical officials, necessary for the performance of certain specified ritual functions, baptism, confirmation, marriage, burial and other sacraments. From the sixth century onwards, most of the recorded bishops were monks, detached from their abbeys to serve the needs of the laity. As monks, they remained subject to the authority of their abbot, whose superior

11

rank was so marked that Irish idiom commonly described the Pope as 'abbot of Rome' and Christ as 'abbot of Heaven'.

The peculiarities of the Irish church did not disturb Europe so long as they were confined to Ireland. But Irish missionary zeal was continuously renewed, and soon spilled abroad. In the middle of the seventh century, Irish monks converted the Northumbrian and midland English, who then held suzerainty over the south; and monasteries on the Irish model were permanently implanted upon the English in large numbers. Irish and English monks emigrated in large numbers to Europe, where their fervent piety aroused a response as enthusiastic as at home. Monasteries were founded in large numbers in eastern Gaul, with a few in Italy, by Irish and English immigrants and their native converts, and English and Irish monks successfully undertook the conversion of the pagan Germans and Slavs beyond the Rhine to Christianity.

The eruption of the Irish church into Europe brought its differences from Rome into sharp and controversial focus. Rome demanded conformity. Dispute was wisely centred upon externals, notably the method of calculating the date of Easter, and the form of the tonsure; concentration upon the relatively simple external issues enabled common-sense flexible compromise to be reached upon the essentials, particularly upon ecclesiastical organisation, upon the relation of abbot and bishop to each other and to Rome, and upon the relation of monk and layman to the priest and God.

Each country worked out with time and difficulty its own solution. Among the English, the remains of Roman towns enabled archbishop Theodore to establish an urban see in each main kingdom, and to achieve harmonious relations between bishops, abbots and kings; in most of Wales, where Roman towns were few, the abbots of principal monasteries were accepted simultaneously as the bishops of main kingdoms. But the problems of Ireland were more complicated; and their solution caused the revival and elevation of Patrick's memory.

The ecclesiastical conflicts of the seventh century reflected the ancient antagonism of the north and the south, between Conn's Half (Connaught and Ulster, with Meath), and Mog's Half (Munster and Leinster). The adherents of conformity with Rome quickly won a large following in the south, for Irishmen who frequently travelled to Europe soon learnt the practical disadvantages of insular eccentricity; but the spread of Romanism in the south hardened conservatism in the north. The southerners soon realised that their episcopate was out of step with Europe because their many sees were unfixed, and their bishops owed no allegiance to a metropolitan archbishop, but were each subject to their own abbot.

The first attempt at organisational conformity was advanced by Muirchu's father, Cogitosus, about 650 or a little earlier. He published a biography of Brigit of Kildare in Leinster, the principal saint of the south. His preface proclaims that her bishop, Conlaed, with his heirs after him, was properly 'archbishop of all the churches of Ireland from sea to sea'.[18]

The claim of a Leinster bishop, dependent upon a powerful abbess, to be archbishop of all Ireland had no chance of acceptance in the north, and is not again repeated. But shortly afterwards another Leinster bishop, Aed of Sletty, advanced a subtler and more practicable proposal. He placed his own church under the suzerainty of Armagh. He was a leading advocate of conformity with Rome, and the initiative that presented a northern see, in the centre of conservative resistance, at the head of the conformist movement, was an effective step in winning northern agreement. An immediate by-product of Aed's initiative was Muirchu's biography; for Muirchu asserts that he wrote under the direction of Aed and at his command.

Muirchu's *Life of Patrick* was written in the early stages of the campaign to win the north, and made no extravagant claims. In a plain factual narrative, as accurate as half forgotten memories could permit, he focussed attention upon a single self-evident truth, that the Irish church had been founded by Patrick, long before the time of the monasteries; and that Patrick was a properly consecrated Roman bishop, trained by the orthodox Germanus, appointed as the immediate and legitimate successor of Palladius, whom the Pope had personally consecrated. His narrative concentrates upon Patrick's origins and arrival and is simplified by reaching a climax with Patrick's triumph at Tara, the traditional centre of the High King of Ireland. The account of the High King's formal conversion did duty for the conversion of Ireland and avoided much troublesome further detail.

The Leinster initiative succeeded, and effective agreement with the north was reached at a synod convened at Birr in central Ireland in 697, under the presidency of Adomnan, abbot of Iona and biographer of Columba, at which Aed, Muirchu, and many northern ecclesiastics were present. The Romanists prevailed, but their triumph took long to consolidate. Several churchmen and monasteries long witheld consent; even Adomnan failed to persuade his own monks, who did not yield for another 20 years.

Consolidation needed more forceful argument. Muirchu went on to stress the foundation of Armagh. It was the centre of Patrician tradition, for no important permanent monastery remained at Patrick's own headquarters at Saul, and Armagh was his only other known important personal foundation. But the organisation of a hierarchy under a metropolitan archbishop of Armagh required much more forceful and colourful argument than Muirchu's sober historical narrative. The pioneer of Armagh's wide claim was a contemporary Connaught cleric, Tirechan. His work begins with a very brief condensed summary of Muirchu's narrative, or of Muirchu's sources, and proceeds to audacious assertions, claiming that Patrick was responsible for the foundation of all churches throughout Ireland that did not belong to the major monasteries, and of many that did. He opens with the direct statement that Patrick consecrated 450 bishops and innumerable priests, though neither Patrick himself nor Muirchu suggests that he consecrated any bishops in Ireland; and by himself he had not the power to consecrate any. The rest of the work consists of a long list of churches, set in the framework of a mythical journey of Patrick through Ireland. The method is simple and uniform. Tirechan reports the tradition of each church about its own founders, and makes Patrick baptise them, bless them in youth, foretell their greatness, or otherwise assume responsibility for their foundation. The conclusion is that all these churches owed their origin to Patrick, and should therefore accept the supremacy of his successor at Armagh.

Tirechan's purpose is roundly stated. 'If Patrick's heir should claim his parish, he could recover almost the whole island, for God gave it him . . . for his are all the early churches of Ireland'. But he admits that the claim is not believed by contemporaries, for his heart was troubled to see that 'deserters and rogues and military men bear hatred to the parish of Patrick, since they have taken from it what was his.'[19] The 'deserters and rogues' were churchmen who did not admit the claims of Patrick's heir at Armagh, and denied the truth of Tirechan's assertions. They were of course right. Patrick did not consecrate 450, or 50 or any other number of bishops; and most of the people whom Tirechan makes him meet were not born until long after his death.

It is a well known axiom of political deceit that if a lie is to be believed, it must be an outrageous untruth, conceived on a grand scale. Tirechan's pretence was as widely accepted as Geoffrey of Monmouth's pretended History of Britain, and has held sway over men's minds even longer. It was followed in succeeding centuries by a riot of even wilder invention elaborating upon his theme. The earlier of these texts were bound together in the Book of Armagh at the beginning of the 9th century, and became the sacred foundation of the claims of the see. They have ever since pervaded, corrupted and obscured the straightforward reality of his life and work, and would have altogether submerged him if the Armagh Book had not also preserved his own works.

The general body of falsehood produced many significant sidecurrents. One of the more pernicious was an exercise of pedantic Irish scholarship concerning Patrick's age. It began with a figure that the mid-seventh century hermit Constans of Lough Oughter in County Cavan 'discovered in Gaul', to the effect that Patrick 'taught for 61 years'.[20] It was evidently originally a note of his age at death. To it was added the figure, already known to Muirchu, that he studied for 40 years, clearly originally meaning the lapse of time between his arrival at Auxerre and his death. The further addition of the 20 odd years of youth before he reached Auxerre gave a round figure total of 120 years. By the end of the 7th century, a note attached to

Tirechan's book pointed out that this was also the age of Moses; and simple division divided Patrick's life into 60 years spent before he reached Ireland, and 60 in Ireland.

These abtruse calculations were soon incorporated into the tradition of the annalists. Their arid calculation subtracted 120 years from Patrick's death date, at about 460, and entered his birth at about 340, while another scholar added the 60 years of his life in Ireland to the date of his arrival in 432, to achieve an additional death date at 493. Most Annals thenceforth carried two alternative dates for Patrick's death, and prompted the intelligent Tirechan, or his annotator, to infer that since two different dates were given, there must have been two Patricks,[21] of whom the earlier should be identified with Palladius, the later with the Patrick who landed in 432 and died in 493.

Such mechanical quirks are a normal part of early medieval scholarship. But they experienced an unusual and bizarre revival in the 1940s and 1950s, when a variety of conflicting theories solemnly resurrected the two Patricks, each theory selecting such limited portions of the available evidence as suited its conclusion. These curious speculations, largely confined to Ireland, were scrutinised in a magisterial article in 1962 which exposed their fragile argumentation.[22]

The mass of rubbish that has been piled about the memory of Patrick in ancient and modern times has done little positive harm, for Patrick is his own truthful witness, and Muirchu was a sober biographer. But negative damage has been considerable. Because the extravagance of Tirechan and his successors has been taken as serious evidence for the life of Patrick, who remains the patron saint of Ireland, their true importance has been undervalued; for though they contribute nothing but untruth and distortion to the study of Patrick and the fifth century, they are contemporary texts of the first importance for the history of 7th and 8th century Ireland and its beliefs. They take their place beside a great quantity of secular texts, of equal importance, but equally little studied. These texts deserve full examination, for in these centuries the detailed history of Ireland is considerably better documented than the history of England, or of most European countries; these are the years when Ireland was in the course of transformation from an alien barbarian island into a European nation, and in which all Europe was deeply indebted to the ferment of ideas that poured from Ireland. The neglected texts, misused for the wrong purpose, require proper consideration. They form a proper and significant part of the study of the formation of medieval Europe.

All this literature, important in its own right and its proper context, must be cleared away from the study of Patrick. His own writings and Muirchu's Life, combined with what else is known of the age in which he lived, together give a clear outline of his life and work. To understand them, it is necessary to explain their context and to remove the irrelevance and confusion that hides them. When they can be seen in their own right, Patrick's own awkward language speaks for itself. His courage and his fears, his resolution and his hesitations, his persistent devotion to a people whom he knew, understood and loved, and his determination to do all he could for their well-being on earth and hereafter, in disregard of all obstacles and all other considerations, are utterly remote from the ecclesiastical portrait of a plaster saint and a national idol. He is one of the few personalities of fifth century Europe who has revealed himself with living warmth, in terms that men of any age who care for their fellows can comprehend. He is no more typical of his time than any other man in any other time; but through the eyes of Patrick men may penetrate beyond the headlines and the generalities of historians ancient and modern, may perceive something of the human problems that are common to their age and his and also something of the essential differences that distinguish one age from the other. Patrick's moving and intensely personal account of his life and troubles is much more than a story of the conversion of the Irish to Christianity; it touches the mainsprings of human endeavour and teaches not only the history of one period, but the substance of what history is about.

JOHN MORRIS

NOTES

1. For further discussion of the historical evidence see J. Morris 'The dates of the Celtic Saints' *Journal of Theological Studies* N.S. 17 (1966), 342 - 391; and, more generally, J. Morris *The Age of Arthur* (London, 1973). Other treatments of the controversies surrounding Patrick are most easily accessible in the following: L. Bieler *The Life and Legend of St. Patrick* (Dublin, 1948); D. A. Binchy 'Patrick and his biographers' *Studia Hibernica* 2 (1962), 7 - 173; R. P. C. Hanson *St. Patrick: his Origins and Career* (Oxford, 1968).
2. J. F. Kenney *Sources for the Early History of Ireland* (New York, 1929), p. 324.
3. *Dicta* 1.
4. Sulpicius Severus *Vita S. Martini* 9.
5. Muirchu 1.9.
6. *Confessio* 23.
7. *Confessio* 23.
8. Prosper of Aquitaine *Chronicle*, ed. Mommsen: M.G.H. Auct. Ant. ix, p.472.
9. *Ibid.*, p. 473.
10. Prosper of Aquitaine *Contra Collatorem* 21 (PL 51.271).
11. Muirchu 1.8.
12. cf. J. Morris *The Age of Arthur*, pp. 62-66.
13. Muirchu 1.10.
14. *Confessio* 26-27.
15. *Confessio* 13.
16. Muirchu 1.23.
17. Muirchu 1.25.
18. Cogitosus *Vita S. Brigittae: Acta Sanctorum* Feb. i, p. 135.
19. Tirechan *Collectanea*: Book of Armagh, fol. 11 a 2; ed. Hogan *Analecta Bollandiana* 2 (1883), pp. 45-46.
20. Book of Armagh, fol. 8 b 2; ed. Hogan *Analecta Bollandiana* 1 (1882),p.584.
21. Tirechan *Collectanea*: Book of Armagh, fol. 16 a 1; ed. Hogan, p. 67.
22. D. A. Binchy *Studia Hibernica* 2 (1962), pp. 7-173.

PREFACE

1. *THE WRITINGS OF ST. PATRICK*

Of the letters and other documents written by Patrick only two survive whose authenticity is unquestionable; they are conventionally termed the *Confessio* ('Declaration') and the *Epistola* ('Letter'). A small group of 'Sayings' of the saint, the *Dicta Patricii*, may also be genuine, at least in part.

The definitive critical edition of these works was published with a linguistic commentary in 1950-1951 by L. Bieler.[1] The earliest manuscript is the Book of Armagh (A), which was written at Armagh early in the 9th century; there is a colophon by the scribe Ferdomnach datable to 807. 'A' includes the 'Declaration', with some omissions, and the 'Sayings' in a collection of Patrician documents; but it does not contain the 'Letter'.

The other main stream of the textual tradition is represented by six manuscripts of the 10th to 12th centuries, containing both 'Declaration' and 'Letter' except where noted. These are:

P: Paris B. N. lat. 17626 10th century

V: Arras Bibl. Mun. 450 12th century. Two leaves are missing; a 17th century copy for the Bollandists (v) reproduces them, with dubious accuracy.

R: Rouen Bibl. Mun. 1391 11th century. Contains part of 'Declaration' only.

F: Oxford Bodl. Fell 3 12th century

C: London B. M. Cotton
Nero E.1 *c.* 1000

G: Oxford Bodl. Fell 4 11th/12th century

In addition, indirect evidence for constituting the text of Patrick can be gained from subsequent biographies of Patrick, which naturally drew on the saint's own writings.

The *Confessio* is the more substantial of Patrick's two works. It is not essentially a confession of sins but rather a declaration of his personal mission to the Irish and a confession of praise and gratitude to the God who called him to that mission. Written to counter criticisms, it is a humble but powerful statement in justification of his work in Ireland; hence the fine concluding phrase: 'and this is my declaration before I die'.

The shorter *Epistola* is an indignant protest against the outrages committed on Irish Christians in a raid by soldiers of the British king Coroticus; some had been butchered, others taken prisoner. It is a second appeal for their release and is addressed to the soldiers of Coroticus, to be read out before the king and his people. But it is very much of an open letter; besides the direct address to Coroticus and to his soldiers, and the emotional apostrophe to those martyred in the raid, Patrick appeals to all right-minded Christians to have nothing to do with those involved in the atrocity. He calls down divine vengeance on the culprits and again emphasises his vocation as apostle to the Irish, despite critics in his home country.

Repeatedly Patrick draws attention to his own lack of learning and culture, to the 'rusticity' of his Latin. For once this is not the Christian Latin author's deliberate choice of the 'lowly style' (*sermo humilis*); nor is it the conventional self-abasing apology for poor style and grammatical inaccuracy even when neither is present. Patrick is struggling to express himself in a language which he has never wholly mastered. Latin had been a second language to him in childhood and his literary education was abruptly terminated when he was captured by Irish raiders at the age of sixteen.[2] There is no certain reminiscence of any Latin author, Christian or secular, in his writing; the only book which he can be seen to know is the Latin Bible, which he quotes freely and which provides him with much of his vocabulary and phraseology. The text printed here identifies and puts within quotation marks only those biblical phrases or sentences which Patrick consciously quotes, introducing them by some such formula as 'it is written'; but there are numerous others which are incorporated into the movement of his prose.

Besides the pervasive influence of the Bible and liturgy, Patrick shows many features of the colloquial Latin of his period. His usage of cases and inflexions, of word-forms, of pronouns and of particles had something in common with other late Latin writers at a popular level. But while colloquial and biblical Latin tend to string phrases together and to avoid subordination of clauses, the process has gone farther in Patrick. His sentence structure often breaks down completely, as one clause tumbles after another; and when he does attempt to subordinate one idea to another, the result can be syntactical conflation and confusion. In the 'Letter' exclamation and parenthesis give an impression of spluttering incoherence and indignation. Throughout, the reader feels that Patrick is hampered by poverty of vocabulary and inadequate command of the structure of the Latin sentence. As Patrick flounders, the result is sometimes not only disorganisation but real obscurity.

To draw conclusions from Patrick's unique Latin is, however, problematic. We lack the appropriate contemporary comparative material at this sub-literary level, from Britain or from Gaul. It has been shown[3] that British Latin pronunciation was more conservative than on the Continent, but any surviving British Latin texts of the period are polished literary products and throw no light on the spoken language. The colloquial elements in Patrick's style could have come from a period of his life spent among Latin speakers either in Britain or in Gaul—or both; though it is probable that Celtic was more dominant in Britain than in central France, where the Gaulish language was moribund by the 5th century. In any case, the question is complicated by Patrick's quite exceptional circumstances. Not only was his Latin education in Britain interrupted; in his later years spent as bishop in Ireland he may be supposed to have used Latin rarely outside a restricted ecclesiastical context. Perhaps the only clear evidence which Patrick's Latin affords is negative; the complete absence of the terminology especially associated with the monasticism of Lérins suggests that he did not spend any appreciable time in such circles.

Patrick's Latin is often compared with that of the pilgrim Egeria, who wrote an account of her pilgrimage to the East early in the 5th century for the benefit of the pious sisters at home in north-west Spain or southern France. Her language is colloquial, and she too is repetitious and illogical in her sentence structure; but there is a blandness and a fluency in her writing which contrasts markedly with Patrick's. Whereas she is writing unselfconsciously in a Latin closely related to, if not identical with, her everyday speech, Patrick is composing neither in his own native Brittonic nor in the Irish of his adopted home; hence his artlessness and his groping for the right Latin expression.

Patrick's *Confessio* cannot even approach the very different *Confessiones* of Augustine of Hippo, whose verbal brilliance is occasionally in danger of being no more than words. Yet Patrick has more to say than he has words in which to express himself, and there is an attraction and vividness in his Latin's 'dynamic clumsiness, or clumsy dynamism'.[4]

2.   MUIRCHU'S LIFE OF ST. PATRICK

The earliest and most reliable extant Latin biography of Patrick was written by Muirchu in the later 7th century. The establishment of a text bristles with difficulties; as with so many medieval compositions the tradition is more fluid than in the case of hallowed classical or patristic works. The text here is again based on the Book of Armagh (A) and reproduces Book 1 as defined in that manuscript (folios 2-7); this takes the story of Patrick from his infancy through to the beginning of his mission in Ireland, his clash with King Loegaire at Tara and his foundation of Armagh. The narrative is expanded in Book 2 (A) by additional miracles and information and by the death of Patrick.

In fact the book division varies in the manuscript tradition. There is a good case for a book division after ch. 22 (A), with Patrick, having overcome the king's opposition, now setting out on his work; the second book would then cover Armagh and other tales, and the third concentrate mainly on the end of the saint's life. In the face of defective manuscripts and varying chapter arrangement it is difficult to decide whether these three sections were initially conceived as a unity, but there is no reason to think that they were not all written by Muirchu. On the other hand the list of chapter headings in 'A' indicates that Book 1 (A) was, at least in some versions, regarded as an independent whole, and it is that list which has been used, for the sake of consistency, as the framework for the present text.

But 'A' does not contain the whole of Muirchu Book 1; folio 1 is now lost as a result of the use of the open volume for oaths and for the production of miraculous water; therefore ch. 1-7 (*init.*) are missing. Ch. 27-29 are also omitted from the text in 'A', but a contemporary scribe added (from another manuscript?) the preface and chapter-headings for Book 1 (A) at folio 20, after further items in Patrick's dossier; and the chapter-headings for ch. 27-29 are included there.

Two other manuscripts have a recension of Muirchu substantially similar to 'A': the Vienna fragment, Vienna Bibl. Nat. ser. nova 3642 (C), and Brussels Bibl. Reg. 64 (B).

'C' consists of two folios of late 8th century date. It contains ch. 8-11 (. . . *et venerunt aliquantulum*), and, in a mutilated state, ch. 19 (*mirabilis episcopus . . . *.)-22. Like B it begins Book 2 after ch. 22, and a few words of the linking sentence as in B (ch. 27 *init.*) are preserved.

'B' is of the 11th century. It contains ch. 1-22, preceded by a garbled prologue which combines notes on Patrick with details about Basil of Caesarea. It continues, as its second book, with ch. 27, 29, 28, 23, 24, 25—breaking off in the middle of that chapter (. . . *et portate illam vobiscum*).

A freer and more fluent version of Muirchu is contained in Novara Bibl. cap. 77 (N), of the 13th century. It represents the only complete text of Muirchu, but the reworking has been considerable. There is no preface and no book division. In addition to these primary sources for the text, other lives of Patrick incorporate passages from Muirchu, with varying degrees of literalness. These are the *Vita secunda* (V2), *Vita tertia* (V3), and *Vita quarta* (V4);[5] and Probus *Life of St. Patrick* (P).

The first critical edition of Muirchu was by E. Hogan in *Analecta Bollandiana* 1 (1882) 531-585. The manuscripts have been published as follows:

A: introduction and transcript: J. Gwynn *Liber Ardmachanus* (Dublin, 1913); facsimile: E. J. Gwynn *The Book of Armagh: the Patrician Documents* (Dublin, 1937).

B: transcript: J. Gwynn *Liber Ardmachanus* 443-451.

C: ed. L. Bieler *Proceedings of the Royal Irish Academy* 59C (1957-59) 181-195.

N: ed. L. Bieler *Proceedings of the Royal Irish Academy* 52C (1948-50) 179-220.

V2, V3, V4, P: ed. L. Bieler *Four Latin Lives of St. Patrick* (Scriptores Latini Hiberniae 8; Dublin, 1971).

Only a tentative reconstruction of the text of Muirchu is possible here. A is used as the foundation, and its evidence is supplemented from elsewhere only when the manuscript is physically defective or the sense and Latinity suspect.

Muirchu's writing is very different from that of his hero.[6] Muirchu has stylistic pretensions, which fortunately do not permeate the whole work. In general, his diction is less precious than that of his contemporary Adomnan, the biographer of St. Columba; and he does not indulge in Adomnan's intricate, interweaving word-order. Muirchu can tell an anecdote in direct terms; the episodes with Dichu and Miliucc (ch. 11-12) or Daire (ch. 25) are straight-forward accounts with easy use of participles for fluency and direct speech for vividness.

But Muirchu's style can have a curiously clotted texture. The early chapters are in places compressed and almost breathless in their piling up of words, often without connectives. In particular, he has a weakness for long strings of balancing participial or adjectival phrases, as in the prophecy of the effects of Patrick's mission on Ireland (ch. 10) or the description of the villainous robber Macuil (ch. 23). Moreover, in common with most medieval hagiographers, he looks for biblical parallels to the events described. But while some biographers will allow such scriptural analogues to shape the story subtly and unobtrusively, Muirchu points the comparisons most explicitly;[7] as a result they tend to intrude clumsily in the flow of the narrative, as do his explanatory asides on places mentioned.

Muirchu is not uneducated, and he slips in a quotation from Vergil and from Sedulius in Book 2 (A). But even if we make allowances for the poor state of the text, in, for example, ch. 27-28, it is clear that Muirchu has not achieved an homogeneous narrative style. At times his striving after what he regards as fine writing becomes apparent, particularly in the preface, which carefully observes the niceties of humility and deference to one's superior in a series of ablative phrases. The preface also exploits the metaphor of embarking upon the work as though upon a stormy sea—a well-worn rhetorical image used also by the 7th-century biographer of St. Samson of Dol and by Cogitosus, perhaps Muirchu's father, in his *Life of St. Brigit*; but Muirchu over-elaborates it to the point·of bombast. Muirchu has a good grasp of the Latin language, but his style lacks elegance and consistency.

University of Edinburgh   ALLAN HOOD

NOTES

1.   'Libri Epistolarum Sancti Patricii Episcopi: Introduction, text and commentary by Ludwig Bieler. *Classica et Mediaevalia* 11 (1950) 1-150; 12 (1951) 81-214.

21

2. *Confessio* 9-12.
3. K. Jackson *Language and History in Early Britain* (Edinburgh, 1953) ch. 3.
4. C. Mohrmann *The Latin of St. Patrick* (Dublin, 1961), p. 33.
5. so numbered in the edition by J. Colgan *Trias Thaumaturga* (Louvain, 1647).
6. see now L. Bieler 'Muirchu's Life of St. Patrick as a work of literature' *Medium Aevum* 43 (1974) 219-233.
7. e.g. ch. 13 the first Passover in Egypt/the first Easter in Ireland; ch. 15 Nebuchadnezzar at Babylon/Loegaire at Tara; ch. 28 St. Stephen/St. Patrick.

CONFESSIO

1 Ego Patricius, peccator rusticissimus et minimus omnium fidelium et contemptibilissimus apud plurimos, patrem habui Calpornium diaconum, filium quondam Potiti presbyteri*, qui fuit vico Bannavem Taberniae; villulam enim prope habuit, ubi ego capturam dedi. Annorum eram tunc fere sedecim. Deum enim verum ignorabam et Hiberione in captivitate adductus sum cum tot milia hominum, secundum merita nostra, quia a Deo recessimus et praecepta eius non custodivimus et sacerdotibus nostris non oboedientes fuimus, qui nostram salutem admonebant; et Dominus induxit super nos iram animationis suae et dispersit nos in gentibus multis etiam usque ad ultimum terrae, ubi nunc parvitas mea esse videtur inter alienigenas.

2 Et ibi Dominus aperuit sensum incredulitatis meae, ut vel sero rememorarem delicta mea et ut converterem toto corde ad Dominum Deum meum, qui respexit humilitatem meam et misertus est adolescentiae et ignorantiae meae et custodivit me antequam scirem eum et antequam saperem vel distinguerem inter bonum et malum et munivit me et consolatus est me ut pater filium.

3 Unde autem tacere non possum — neque expedit quidem — tanta beneficia et tantam gratiam quam mihi Dominus praestare dignatus est in terra captivitatis meae; quia haec est retributio nostra, ut post correptionem vel agnitionem Dei exaltare et confiteri mirabilia eius coram omni natione quae est sub omni caelo;

4 quia non est alius Deus nec umquam fuit nec ante nec erit post haec praeter Deum Patrem, ingenitum, sine principio, a quo est omne principium, omnia tenentem, ut didicimus;* et huius filium Iesum Christum, quem cum Patre scilicet semper fuisse testamur, ante originem saeculi spiritaliter apud Patrem, inenarrabiliter genitum ante omne principium; et per ipsum facta sunt visibilia et invisibilia; hominem factum, morte devicta in caelis ad Patrem receptum; et dedit illi omnem potestatem super omne nomen caelestium et terrestrium et infernorum, ut omnis lingua confiteatur ei quia Dominus et Deus est Iesus Christus, quem credimus et expectamus adventum ipsius mox futurum, iudex vivorum atque mortuorum, qui reddet unicuique secundum facta sua; et effudit in nobis habunde Spiritum Sanctum,

donum et pignus immortalitatis, qui facit credentes et oboedientes ut sint filii Dei et coheredes Christi; quem confitemur et adoramus unum Deum in Trinitate sancti nominis.

5   Ipse enim dixit per prophetam: 'Invoca me in die tribulationis tuae et liberabo te et magnificabis me.' Et iterum inquit: 'Opera autem Dei revelare et confiteri honorificum est.'

6   Tamen etsi in multis imperfectus sum, opto fratribus et cognatis meis scire qualitatem meam, ut possint perspicere votum animae meae.

7   Non ignoro testimonium Domini mei, qui in psalmo testatur: 'Perdes eos qui loquuntur mendacium.' Et iterum inquit: 'Os quod mentitur occidit animam.' Et idem Dominus in evangelio inquit: 'Verbum otiosum quod locuti fuerint homines, reddent pro eo rationem in die iudicii.'

8   Unde autem vehementer debueram cum timore et tremore metuere hanc sententiam in die illa ubi nemo se poterit subtrahere vel abscondere, sed omnes omnino reddituri sumus rationem etiam minimorum peccatorum ante tribunal Domini Christi.

9   Quapropter olim cogitavi scribere, sed et usque nunc haesitavi; timui enim ne incederem in linguam hominum, quia non didici sicut et ceteri, qui optime itaque iura * et sacras litteras utraque pari modo combiberunt et sermones illorum ex infantia numquam mutarunt, sed magis ad perfectum semper addiderunt. Nam sermo et loquela nostra translata est in linguam alienam, sicut facile potest probari ex saliva scripturae meae qualiter sum ego in sermonibus instructus atque eruditus, quia, inquit, 'sapiens per linguam dinoscetur, et sensus et scientia et doctrina veritatis.'

10 Sed quid prodest excusatio iuxta veritatem, praesertim cum praesumptione quatenus modo ipse adpeto in senectute mea quod in iuventute non comparavi, quod obstiterunt peccata mea ut confirmarem quod ante perlegeram? Sed quis me credit etsi dixero quod ante praefatus sum? Adolescens, immo paene puer imberbis, * capturam dedi, antequam scirem quid adpeterem vel quid vitare debueram. Unde ergo hodie erubesco et vehementer pertimeo denudare imperitiam meam, quia ⟨non⟩ disertus* brevitate sermonem* explicare nequeo, sicut enim spiritus gestit et animus et sensus monstrat effectus.

11 Sed si itaque datum mihi fuisset sicut et ceteris, verumtamen non silerem propter retributionem, et si forte videtur apud aliquantos me in hoc praeponere cum mea inscientia et tardiori lingua, sed etiam

(scriptum est enim): 'Linguae balbutientes velociter discent loqui pacem.' Quanto magis nos adpetere debemus, qui sumus, inquit, 'epistola Christi in salutem usque ad ultimum terrae,' et si non deserta sed †ratum et fortissimum† 'scripta in cordibus vestris non atramento sed Spiritu Dei vivi.' Et iterum Spiritus testatur et rusticationem ab Altissimo creatam.

12 Unde ego primus rusticus profuga indoctus scilicet, qui nescio in posterum providere, sed illud scio certissime quia utique priusquam humiliarer ego eram velut lapis qui iacet in luto profundo; et venit qui potens est et in sua misericordia sustulit me et quidem scilicet sursum adlevavit et collocavit me in summo pariete; et inde fortiter debueram exclamare ad retribuendum quoque aliquid Domino pro tantis beneficiis eius hic et in aeternum, quae mens hominum aestimare non potest.

13 Unde autem ammiramini itaque, magni et pusilli qui timetis Deum, et vos, dominicati * rethorici, audite et scrutamini. Quis me stultum excitavit de medio eorum qui videntur esse sapientes et legis periti et potentes in sermone et in omni re, et me quidem, detestabilis huius mundi, prae ceteris inspiravit si talis essem (dummodo autem!) ut cum metu et reverentia et sine querella fideliter prodessem genti ad quam caritas Christi transtulit et donavit me in vita mea, si dignus fuero; denique ut cum humilitate et veraciter deservirem illis.

14 In mensura itaque fidei Trinitatis oportet distinguere, sine reprehensione periculi notum facere donum Dei et consolationem aeternam, sine timore fiducialiter Dei nomen ubique expandere, ut etiam post obitum meum exagaellias relinquere fratribus et filiis meis quos in Domino ego baptizavi tot milia hominum.

15 Et non eram dignus neque talis ut hoc Dominus servulo suo concederet, post aerumnas et tantas moles, post captivitatem, post annos multos in gentem illam tantam gratiam mihi donaret — quod ego aliquando in iuventute mea nunquam speravi neque cogitavi.

16 Sed postquam Hiberione deveneram, cotidie itaque pecora pascebam et frequens in die orabam; magis ac magis accedebat amor Dei et timor ipsius et fides augebatur et spiritus agebatur, ut in die una usque ad centum orationes et in nocte prope similiter, ut etiam in silvis et monte manebam, et ante lucem excitabar ad orationem per nivem, per gelu, per pluviam, et nihil mali sentiebam neque ulla pigritia erat in me — sicut modo video, quia tunc Spiritus in me fervebat.

17 Et ibi scilicet quadam nocte in somno audivi vocem dicentem mihi:
'Bene ieiunas cito iturus ad patriam tuam;' et iterum post paululum
tempus audivi responsum dicentem mihi: 'Ecce navis tua parata est.'
Et non erat prope, sed forte habebat ducenta milia passus et ibi
numquam fueram nec ibi notum quemquam de hominibus habebam.
Et deinde postmodum conversus sum in fugam et intermisi hominem
cum quo fueram sex annis et veni in virtute Dei, qui viam meam ad
bonum dirigebat (et nihil metuebam), donec perveni ad navem illam.

18 Et illa die qua perveni profecta est navis de loco suo, et locutus sum
ut haberum unde navigare cum illis; et gubernator displicuit illi et
acriter cum indignatione respondit: 'Nequaquam tu nobiscum adpetes
ire.' Et cum haec audiissem, separavi me ab illis ut venirem ad
tegoriolum ubi hospitabam, et in itinere coepi orare et antequam
orationem consummarem audivi unum ex illis, et fortiter exclamabat
post me: 'Veni cito, quia vocant te homines isti,' et statim ad illos
reversus sum, et coeperunt mihi dicere: 'Veni quia ex fide recipimus
te; fac nobiscum amicitiam quo modo volueris' (et in illa die itaque
reppuli sugere mamellas eorum propter timorem Dei, sed verumtamen
ab illis speravi venire in fidem Iesu Christi, quia gentes erant), et ob
hoc obtinui cum illis, et protinus navigavimus.

19 Et post triduum terram cepimus et viginti octo dies per desertum
iter fecimus, et cibus defuit illis et fames invaluit super eos, et alio
die coepit gubernator mihi dicere: 'Quid est, Christiane? Tu dicis
deus tuus magnus et omnipotens est; quare ergo non potes pro nobis
orare? Quia nos a fame periclitamur; difficile est enim ut aliquem
hominem umquam videamus.' Ego enim confidenter dixi illis:
'Convertimini ex fide, ex toto corde ad Dominum Deum meum,
quia nihil est impossibile illi, ut hodie cibum mittat vobis in viam
vestram usque dum satiamini; quia ubique habundat illi.' Et adiuvante
Deo ita factum est; ecce grex porcorum in via ante oculos nostros
apparuit, et multos ex illis interfecerunt et ibi duas noctes manserunt
et bene refecti et carne * eorum repleti sunt, quia multi ex illis
defecerunt et secus viam semivivi relicti sunt; et post hoc summas
gratias egerunt Deo, et ego honorificatus sum sub oculis eorum, et ex
hac die cibum habundanter habuerunt. Etiam mel silvestre invenerunt
et mihi partem obtulerunt et unus ex illis dixit: 'Immolaticium est.'
Deo gratias, exinde nihil gustavi.

20 Eadem vero nocte eram dormiens, et fortiter temptavit me Satanas,
quod memor ero quamdiu fuero in hoc corpore; et cecidit super me
veluti saxum ingens et nihil membrorum meorum praevalui. Sed unde
mihi venit ignarum in spiritum ut Heliam vocarem? Et inter haec vidi
in caelum solem oriri et dum clamarem 'Helia, Helia' viribus meis,

ecce splendor solis illius decidit super me et statim discussit a me omnem gravitudinem; et credo quod a Christo Domino meo subventus sum et Spiritus eius iam tunc clamabat pro me, et spero quod sic erit in die pressurae meae, sicut in evangelio inquit: 'In illa die, ' Dominus testatur, 'non vos estis qui loquimini, sed Spiritus Patris vestri qui loquitur in vobis.'

21 (Et iterum post annos multos adhuc capturam dedi. Ea nocte prima itaque mansi cum illis. Responsum autem divinum audivi dicentem mihi: 'Duobus mensibus eris cum illis.' Quod ita factum est; nocte illa sexagesima liberavit me Dominus de manibus eorum.)

22 Etiam in itinere praevidit nobis cibum et ignem et siccitatem cotidie donec decimo die pervenimus homines. Sicut superius insinuavi, viginti et octo dies per desertum iter fecimus et ea nocte qua pervenimus homines de cibo vero nihil habuimus.

23 Et iterum post paucos annos in Britaniis eram cum parentibus meis, qui me ut filium susceperunt et ex fide rogaverunt me ut vel modo ego post tantas tribulationes quas ego pertuli nusquam ab illis discederem. Et ibi scilicet vidi in visu noctis virum venientem quasi de Hiberione, cui nomen Victoricus, cum epistolis innumerabilibus, et dedit mihi unam ex his et legi principium epistolae continentem 'Vox Hiberionacum,' et cum recitabam principium epistolae putabam ipso momento audire vocem ipsorum qui erant iuxta silvam Focluti quae est prope mare occidentale, et sic exclamaverunt, quasi ex uno ore: 'Rogamus te, sancte puer, ut venias et adhuc ambulas inter nos;' et valde compunctus sum corde et amplius non potui legere et sic expertus sum. Deo gratias, quia post plurimos annos praestitit illis Dominus secundum clamorem illorum.

24 Et alia nocte (nescio, Deus scit, utrum in me an iuxta me) verbis †peritissime,† * quos ego audivi et non potui intellegere, nisi ad extremum orationis sic effiatus est: 'Qui dedit animam suam pro te, ipse est qui loquitur in te; ' et sic expertus sum gaudibundus.

25 Et iterum vidi in me ipsum orantem et eram quasi intra corpus meum et audivi super me, hoc est super interiorem hominem, et ibi fortiter orabat gemitibus, et inter haec stupebam et ammirabam et cogitabam quis esset qui in me orabat, sed ad postremum orationis sic effiatus est ut sit Spiritus, et sic expertus sum et recordatus sum apostolo dicente: 'Spiritus adiuvat infirmitates orationis nostrae; nam quod oremus sicut oportet nescimus; sed ipse Spiritus postulat pro nobis gemitibus inenarrabilibus, quae verbis exprimi non possunt;' et iterum: 'Dominus advocatus noster postulat pro nobis.'

26 Et quando temptatus sum ab aliquantis senioribus meis, qui venerunt et peccata mea contra laboriosum episcopatum meum ⟨obiecerunt⟩, utique illo die fortiter impulsus sum ut caderem hic et in aeternum; sed Dominus pepercit proselito et peregrino propter nomen suum benigne, et valde mihi subvenit in hac conculcatione. Quod in labe et in obprobrium non male deveni, Deum oro ut non illis in peccatum reputetur.

27 Occasionem post annos triginta invenerunt me adversus verbum quod confessus fueram antequam essem diaconus. Propter anxietatem maesto animo insinuavi amicissimo meo quae in pueritia mea una die gesseram, immo in una hora, quia necdum praevalebam. Nescio, Deus scit, si habebam tunc annos quindecim, et Deum vivum non credebam, neque ex infantia mea; sed in morte et in incredulitate mansi donec valde castigatus sum et in veritate humiliatus sum a fame et nuditate, et cotidie.

28 Contra, Hiberione non sponte pergebam, donec prope deficiebam; sed hoc potius bene mihi fuit, qui ex hoc emendatus sum a Domino, et aptavit me ut hodie essem quod aliquando longe 'a me erat, ut ego curam haberem aut satagerem pro salute aliorum, quando autem tunc etiam de me ipso non cogitabam.

29 Igitur in illo die quo reprobatus sum a memoratis supradictis, ad noctem illam vidi in visu noctis ⟨scriptum quod⟩ * scriptum erat contra faciem meam sine honore, et inter haec audivi responsum divinum dicentem mihi: 'Male vidimus faciem designati nudato nomine;' nec sic praedixit: 'Male vidisti' sed 'male vidimus,' [quasi sibi se iunxisset] *, sicut dixit: 'Qui vos tangit quasi qui tangit pupillam oculi mei.'

30 Idcirco gratias ago ei qui me in omnibus confortavit, ut non me impediret a profectione quam statueram et de mea quoque opera quod a Christo Domino meo didiceram, sed magis ex eo sensi in me virtutem non parvam, et fides mea probata est coram Deo et hominibus.

31 Unde autem audenter dico, non me reprehendit conscientia mea hic et in futurum. Teste Deo habeo quia non sum mentitus in sermonibus quos ego retuli vobis.

32 Sed magis doleo pro amicissimo meo cur hoc meruimus audire tale responsum. Cui ego credidi etiam animam! Et comperi ab aliquantis fratribus ante defensionem illam (quod ego non interfui nec in Britanniis eram nec a me oriebatur*) ut et ille in mea absentia

pulsaret pro me; etiam mihi ipse ore suo dixerat: 'Ecce dandus es tu ad gradum episcopatus' — quod non eram dignus. Sed unde venit illi postmodum ut coram cunctis, bonis et malis, et me publice dehonestaret quod ante sponte et laetus indulserat, et Dominus, qui maior omnibus est?

33 Satis dico. Sed tamen non debeo abscondere donum Dei quod largitus est nobis in terra captivitatis meae, quia tunc fortiter inquisivi eum et ibi inveni illum, et servavit me ab omnibus iniquitatibus (sic credo) propter inhabitantem Spiritum eius, qui operatus est usque in hanc diem in me. Audenter rursus; sed scit Deus, si mihi homo hoc effatus fuisset, forsitan tacuissem propter caritatem Christi.

34 .Unde ergo indefessam gratiam ago Deo meo, qui me fidelem servavit in die temptationis meae, ita ut hodie confidenter offeram illi sacrificium ut hostiam viventem animam meam Christo Domino meo, qui me servavit ab omnibus angustiis meis, ut et dicam: quis ego sum, Domine, vel quae est vocatio mea, qui mihi tanta divinitate comparuisti*, ita ut hodie in gentibus constanter exaltarem et magnificarem nomen tuum ubicumque loco fuero, nec non in secundis sed etiam in pressuris, ut quicquid mihi evenerit, sive bonum sive malum, aequaliter debeo suscipere et Deo gratias semper agere, qui mihi ostendit ut indubitalem eum sine fine crederem et qui me adiuverit*, ut ego inscius et in novissimis diebus hoc opus tam pium et tam mirificum auderem adgredere, ita ut imitarem quippiam illos quos ante Dominus iam olim praedixerat praenuntiaturos evangelium suum in testimonium omnibus gentibus ante finem mundi — quod ita ergo vidimus itaque suppletum est; ecce testes sumus quia evangelium praedicatum est usque ubi nemo ultra est.

35 Longum est autem totum per singula enarrare laborem meum vel per partes. Breviter dicam qualiter piissimus Deus de servitute saepe liberavit et de periculis duodecim qua periclitata est anima mea, praeter insidias multas et quae verbis exprimere non valeo. Nec iniuriam legentibus faciam; sed Deum auctorem habeo, qui novit omnia etiam antequam fiant, ut me pauperculum pupillum idiotam* tamen responsum divinum creber admonere.

36 Unde mihi haec sapientia, quae in me non erat, qui nec numerum dierum noveram neque Deum sapiebam? Unde mihi postmodum donum tam magnum, tam salubre, Deum agnoscere vel diligere, sed ut patriam et parentes amitterem?

37 Et munera multa mihi offerebantur cum fletu et lacrimis et offendi

illos, nec non contra votum aliquantis de senioribus meis, sed
gubernante Deo nullo modo consensi neque adquievi illis — non mea
gratia, sed Deus qui vincit in me et resistit illis omnibus, ut ego veneram
ad Hibernas gentes evangelium praedicare et ab incredulis contumelias
perferre, ut audirem obprobrium peregrinationis meae, et persecutiones multas usque ad vincula, et ut darem ingenuitatem meam pro
utilitate aliorum, et, si dignus fuero, promptus sum ut etiam animam
meam incunctanter et libentissime pro nomine eius; et ibi opto
impendere eam usque ad mortem, si Dominus mihi indulgeret,

38   quia valde debitor sum Deo, qui mihi tantam gratiam donavit ut
populi multi per me in Deum renascerentur et postmodum consumm-
arentur et ut clerici ubique illis ordinarentur ad plebem nuper
venientem ad credulitatem, quam sumpsit Dominus ab extremis
terrae, sicut olim promiserat per prophetas suos: 'Ad te gentes venient
ab extremis terrae et dicent: 'Sicut falsa comparaverunt patres nostri
idola et non est in eis utilitas;' ' et iterum: 'Posui te lumen in gentibus
ut sis in salutem usque ad extremum terrae.'

39   Et ibi volo expectare promissum ipsius, qui utique numquam fallit,
sicut in evangelio pollicetur: 'Venient ab oriente et occidente et
recumbent cum Abraam et Isaac et Iacob;' sicut credimus ab omni
mundo venturi sunt credentes.

40   Idcirco itaque oportet quidem bene et diligenter piscare, sicut
Dominus praemonet et docet, dicens: 'Venite post me et faciam vos
fieri piscatores hominum;' et iterum dicit per prophetas: 'Ecce
mitto piscatores et venatores multos, dicit Deus;' et cetera. Unde
autem valde oportebat retia nostra tendere, ita ut multitudo copiosa
et turba Deo caperetur et ubique essent clerici qui baptizarent et
exhortarent populum indigentem et desiderantem, sicut Dominus
inquit in evangelio — ammonet et docet, dicens: 'Euntes ergo nunc
docete omnes gentes, baptizantes eas in nomine Patris et Filii et
Spiritus Sancti, docentes eos observare omnia quaecumque mandavi
vobis; et ecce ego vobiscum sum omnibus diebus usque ad
consummationem saeculi;' et iterum dicit: 'Euntes ergo in mundum
universum praedicate evangelium omni creaturae; qui crediderit et
baptizatus fuerit salvus erit; qui vero non crediderit condempnabitur;'
et iterum: 'Praedicabitur hoc evangelium regni in universo mundo in
testimonium omnibus gentibus et tunc veniet finis;' et item Dominus
per prophetam praenuntiat; inquit: 'Et erit in novissimis diebus,
dicit Dominus, effundam de spiritu meo super omnem carnem et
prophetabunt filii vestri et filiae vestrae et iuvenes vestri visiones
videbunt et seniores vestri somnia somniabunt et quidem super servos
meos et super ancillas meas in diebus illis effundam de spiritu meo et

prophetabunt;' et in Osee dicit: 'Vocabo non plebem meam plebem meam et non misericordiam consecutam misericordiam consecutam. Et erit in loco ubi dictum est: 'Non plebs mea vos;' ibi vocabuntur filii Dei vivi.'

41 Unde autem Hiberione qui numquam notitiam Dei habuerunt, nisi idola et immunda usque nunc semper coluerunt, quomodo nuper facta est plebs Domini et filii Dei nuncupantur, filii Scottorum et filiae regulorum monachi et virgines Christi esse videntur?

42 Et etiam una benedicta Scotta genetiva nobilis pulcherrima adulta erat, quam ego baptizavi; et post paucos dies una causa venit ad nos, insinuavit nobis responsum accepisse a nuntio Dei et monuit eam ut esset virgo Christi et ipsa ⟨et⟩ Deo proximaret. Deo Gratias, sexta ab hac die optime et avidissime arripuit illud quod etiam omnes virgines Dei ita hoc faciunt – non sponte patrum earum, sed et persecutiones patiuntur et improperia falsa a parentibus suis et nihilominus plus augetur numerus (et de genere nostro qui ibi nati sunt nescimus numerum eorum) praeter viduas et continentes. Sed ⟨et illae⟩ *maxime laborant quae servitio detinentur; usque ad terrores et minas assidue perferunt; sed Dominus gratiam dedit multis ex ancillis suis, nam etsi vetantur tamen fortiter imitantur.

43 Unde autem etsi voluero amittere illas et ut pergens in Brittanniis – et libentissime paratus eram quasi ad patriam et parentes; non id solum sed etiam usque ad Gallias visitare fratres et ut viderem faciem sanctorum Domini mei; scit Deus quod ego valde optabam, sed alligatus Spiritu, qui mihi protestatur si hoc fecero ut futurum reum me esse designat, et timeo perdere laborem quem inchoavi – et non ego sed Christus Dominus, qui me imperavit ut venirem esse cum illis residuum aetatis meae, si Dominus voluerit et custodierit me ab omni via mala, ut non peccem coram illo.

44 Spero autem hoc debueram, sed memetipsum non credo quamdiu fuero in hoc corpore mortis, quia fortis est qui cotidie nititur subvertere me a fide et praeposita castitate religionis non fictae usque in finem vitae meae Christo Domino meo; sed caro inimica semper trahit ad mortem, id est ad inlecebras inlicitate perficiendas; et scio ex parte quare vitam perfectam ego non egi sicut et ceteri credentes, sed confiteor Domino meo, et non erubesco in conspectu ipsius, quia non mentior, ex quo cognovi eum a iuventute mea crevit in me amor Dei et timor ipsius, et usque nunc favente Domino fidem servavi.

45 Rideat autem et insultet qui voluerit, ego non silebo neque abscondo

signa et mirabilia quae mihi a Domino monstrata sunt ante multos
annos quam fierent, quasi qui novit omnia etiam ante tempora
saecularia.

46 Unde autem debueram sine cessatione Deo gratias agere, qui saepe
indulsit insipientiae meae, neglegentiae meae, et de loco non in uno
quoque ut non mihi vehementer irasceretur, qui adiutor datus sum
et non cito adquievi secundum quod mihi ostensum fuerat et sicut
Spiritus suggerebat, et misertus est mihi Dominus in milia milium,
quia vidit in me quod paratus eram, sed quod mihi pro his nesciebam
de statu meo quid facerem, quia multi hanc legationem prohibebant,
etiam inter se ipsos pos tergum meum narrabant et dicebant: 'Iste
quare se mittit in periculo inter hostes qui Deum non noverunt?'
Non ut causa malitiae, sed non sapiebat illis, sicut et ego ipse testor —
intellige* propter rusticitatem meam; et non cito agnovi gratiam
quae tunc erat in me; nunc mihi sapit quod ante debueram.

47 Nunc ergo simpliciter insinuavi fratribus et conservis meis qui mihi
crediderunt propter quod praedixi et praedico ad roborandam et
confirmandam fidem vestram. Utinam ut et vos imitemini maiora et
potiora faciatis! Hoc erit gloria mea, quia filius sapiens gloria patris
est.

48 Vos scitis et Deus qualiter inter vos conversatus sum a iuventute mea
in fide veritatis et in sinceritate cordis. Etiam ad gentes illas inter
quas habito, ego fidem illis praestavi et praestabo. Deus scit, neminem
illorum circumveni, nec cogito, propter Deum et ecclesiam ipsius, ne
excitem illis et nobis omnibus persecutionem et ne per me blasphem-
aretur nomen Domini; quia scriptum est: 'Vae homini per quem nomen
Domini blasphematur.'

49 Nam etsi imperitus sum in omnibus, tamen conatus sum quippiam
servare me etiam et fratribus Christianis et virginibus Christi et
mulieribus religiosis, quae mihi ultronea munuscula donabant et
super altare iactabant ex ornamentis suis et iterum reddebam illis
et adversus me scandalizabantur cur hoc faciebam; sed ego propter
spem perennitatis, ut me in omnibus caute propterea conservarem,
ita ut ⟨non⟩ *me in aliquo titulo infideli caperent vel ministerium
servitutis meae nec etiam in minimo incredulis locum darem infamare
sive detractare.

50 Forte autem quando baptizavi tot milia hominum speraverim ab
aliquo illorum vel dimidio scriptulae? Dicite mihi et reddam vobis. Aut
quando ordinavit ubique Dominus clericos per modicitatem meam et
ministerium gratis distribui illis, si poposci ab aliquo illorum vel

pretium vel calciamenti mei, dicite adversus me et reddam vobis.

51 Magis ego impendi pro vobis ut me caperent, et inter vos et ubique pergebam causa vestra in multis periculis etiam usque ad exteras partes, ubi nemo ultra erat et ubi numquam aliquis pervenerat qui baptizaret aut clericos ordinaret aut populum consummaret; donante Domino diligenter et libentissime pro salute vestra omnia generavi.

52 Interim praemia dabam regibus praeter quod dabam mercedem filiis ipsorum qui mecum ambulant, et nihilominus comprehenderunt me cum comitibus meis et illa die avidessime cupiebant interficere me, sed tempus nondum venerat; et omnia quaecumque nobiscum invenerunt rapuerunt illud et me ipsum ferro vinxerunt et quartodecimo die absolvit me Dominus de potestate eorum et quicquid nostrum fuit redditum est nobis propter Deum et necessarios amicos quos ante praevidimus.

53 Vos autem experti estis quantum ego erogavi illis qui iudicabant per omnes regiones quos ego frequentius visitabam. Censeo enim non minimum quam pretium quindecim hominum distribui illis, ita ut me fruamini et ego vobis semper fruar in Deum. Non me paenitet nec satis est mihi; adhuc impendo et superimpendam. Potens est Dominus ut det mihi postmodum ut meipsum impendar pro animabus vestris.

54 Ecce testem Deum invoco in animam meam quia non mentior; neque ut sit occasio adulationis vel avaritiae scripserim vobis neque ut honorem spero ab aliquo vestrum; sufficit enim honor qui nondum videtur sed corde creditur; fidelis autem qui promisit, numquam mentitur.

55 Sed video iam in praesenti saeculo me supra modum exaltatum a Domino, et non eram dignus neque talis ut hoc mihi praestaret, dum scio certissime quod mihi melius convenit paupertas et calamitas quam divitiae et diliciae (sed et Christus Dominus pauper fuit pro nobis, ego vero miser et infelix etsi opes voluero iam non habeo), neque meipsum iudico, quia cotidie spero aut internicionem aut circumveniri aut redigi in servitutem sive occasio cuiuslibet; sed nihil horum vereor propter promissa caelorum, quia iactavi meipsum in manus Dei omnipotentis, qui ubique dominatur; sicut propheta dicit; 'Iacta cogitatum tuum in Deum et ipse te enutriet.'

56 Ecce nunc commendo animam meam fidelissimo Deo meo, pro quo legationem fungor in ignobilitate mea, sed quia personam non accipit et elegit me ad hoc officium ut unus essem de suis minimis minister.

57 Unde autem retribuam illi pro omnibus quae retribuit mihi. Sed quid dicam vel quid promittam Domino meo, quia nihil valeo nisi ipse mihi dederit? Sed scrutator corda et renes, quia satis et nimis cupio et paratus eram ut donaret mihi bibere calicem eius, sicut indulsit et ceteris amantibus se.

58 Quapropter non contingat mihi a Deo meo ut numquam amittam plebem suam quam adquisivit in ultimis terrae. Oro Deum ut det mihi perseverantiam et dignetur ut reddam illi testem fidelem usque ad transitum meum propter Deum meum.

59 Et si aliquid boni umquam imitatus sum propter Deum meum quem diligo, peto illi det mihi ut cum illis proselitis et captivis pro nomine suo effundam sanguinem meum, etsi ipsam etiam caream sepulturam aut miserissime cadaver per singula membra dividatur canibus aut bestiis asperis aut volucres caeli comederent illud. Certissime reor, si mihi hoc incurrisset, lucratus sum animam cum corpore meo, quia sine ulla dubitatione in die illa resurgemus in claritate solis, hoc est in gloria Christi Iesu redemptoris nostri, quasi filii Dei vivi et coheredes Christi et conformes futuri imaginis ipsius; quoniam ex ipso et per ipsum et in ipso regnaturi sumus.

60 Nam sol ist quem videmus ⟨ipso⟩ * iubente propter nos cotidie oritur, sed numquam regnabit neque permanebit splendor eius, sed et omnes qui adorant eum in poenam miseri male devenient; nos autem, qui credimus et adoramus solem verum Christum, qui numquam interibit — neque qui fecerit voluntatem ipsius, sed manebit in aeternum quomodo et Christus manet in aeternum, qui regnat cum Deo Patre omnipotente et cum Spiritu Sancto ante saecula et nunc et per omnia saecula saeculorum, Amen.

61 Ecce iterum iterumque breviter exponam verba confessionis meae. Testificor in veritate et in exultatione cordis coram Deo et sanctis angelis eius quia numquam habui aliquam occasionem praeter evangelium et promissa illius ut umquam redirem ad gentem illam unde prius vix evaseram.

62 Sed precor credentibus et timentibus Deum, quicumque dignatus fuerit inspicere vel recipere hanc scripturam quam Patricius peccator indoctus scilicet Hiberione conscripsit, ut nemo umquam dicat quod mea ignorantia, si aliquid pusillum egi vel demonstraverim secundum Dei placitum, sed arbitramini et verissime credatur quod donum Dei fuisset. Et haec est confessio mea antequam moriar.

EPISTOLA

1 Patricius, peccator indoctus scilicet Hiberione constitutus, episcopum me esse fateor. Certissime reor a Deo accepi id quod sum. Inter barbaras itaque gentes habito, proselitus et profuga ob amorem Dei; testis est ille si ita est. Non quod optabam tam dure et tam aspere aliquid ex ore meo effundere; sed cogor zelo Dei, et veritas Christi excitavit, pro dilectione proximorum atque filiorum, pro quibus tradidi patriam et parentes et animam meam usque ad mortem. Si dignus sum, vivo Deo meo docere gentes, etsi contempnor aliquibus.

2 Manu mea scripsi atque condidi verba ista danda et tradenda, militibus mittenda Corotici — non dico civibus meis neque civibus sanctorum Romanorum sed civibus daemoniorum, ob mala opera ipsorum. Ritu hostili in morte vivunt, socii Scottorum atque Pictorum apostatarumque. Sanguilentos sanguinare* de sanguine innocentium Christianorum, quos ego innumerum numerum* Deo genui atque in Christo confirmavi!

3 Postera die qua crismati neophyti in veste candidi (flagrabat in fronte ipsorum dum crudeliter trucidati atque mactati gladio supradictis), misi epistolam cum sancto presbytero quem ego ex infantia docui, cum clericis, ut nobis aliquid indulgerent de praeda vel de captivis baptizatis quos ceperunt; cachinnos fecerunt de illis.

4 Idcirco nescio quid magis lugeam; an qui interfecti vel quos ceperunt vel quos graviter zabulus inlaqueavit. Perenni poena gehennae pariter cum ipso mancipabuntur*, quia utique qui facit peccatum servus est et filius zabuli nuncupatur.

5 Quapropter resciat omnis homo timens Deum quod a me alieni sunt et a Christo Deo meo, pro quo legationem fungor; patricida, fratricida, lupi rapaces devorantes plebem Domini ut cibum panis, sicut ait: 'Iniqui dissipaverunt legem tuam, Domine,' quam in supremis temporibus Hiberione optime benigne plantaverat, atque instructa erat favente Deo.

6 Non usurpo; partem habeo cum his quos advocavit et praedestinavit evangelium praedicare in persecutionibus non parvis usque ad

extremum terrae, etsi invidet inimicus per tyrannidem Corotici, qui
Deum non veretur nec sacerdotes ipsius, quos elegit et indulsit illis
summam divinam sublimam potestatem, quos ligarent super terram
ligatos esse et in caelis.

7   Unde ergo quaeso plurimum, sancti et humiles corde; adulari talibus
non licet nec cibum nec potum sumere cum ipsis, nec elemosinas
ipsorum recipi debeat, donec crudeliter ⟨per⟩ * paenitentiam
effusis lacrimis satis Deo faciant et liberent servos Dei et ancillas
Christi baptizatas, pro quibus mortuus est et crucifixus.

8   'Dona iniquorum reprobat Altissimus. Qui offert sacrificium ex
substantia pauperum quasi qui victimat filium in conspectu patris
sui.' 'Divitias,' inquit, 'quas congregavit iniuste evomentur de ventre
eius, trahit illum angelus mortis, ira draconum mulcabitur, interficiet
illum lingua colubris, comedit autem eum ignis inextinguibilis.'
Ideoque, 'Vae qui replent se quae non sunt sua;' vel, 'Quid prodest
homini ut totum mundum lucretur et animae suae detrimentum
patiatur?'

9   Longum est per singula discutere vel insinuare, per totam legem
carpere testimonia de tali cupiditate. Avaritia mortale crimen. 'Non
concupisces rem proximi tui. Non occides.' Homicida non potest esse
cum Christo. 'Qui odit fratrem suum homicida adscribitur;' vel, 'Qui
non diligit fratrem suum in morte manet.' Quanto magis reus est qui
manus suas coinquinavit in sanguine filiorum Dei, quos nuper adquisivit in ultimis terrae per exhortationem parvitatis nostrae!

10 Numquid sine Deo vel secundum carnem Hiberione veni? Quis me
compulit? Alligatus sum Spiritu ut non videam aliquem de cognatione
mea. Numquid a me, piam misericordiam quod ago erga gentem illam
qui me aliquando ceperunt et devastaverunt servos et ancillas domus
patris mei? Ingenuus fui secundum carnem; decorione patre nascor.
Vendidi enim nobilitatem meam (non erubesco neque me paenitet)
pro utilitate aliorum. Denique servus sum in Christo genti exterae ob
gloriam ineffabilem perennis vitae quae est in Christo Iesu Domino
nostro.

11 Et si mei me non cognoscunt, propheta in patria sua honorem non
habet. Forte non sumus ex uno ovili neque unum Deum patrem
habemus, sicut ait: 'Qui non est mecum contra me est, et qui non
congregat mecum spargit.' Non convenit; unus destruit, alter aedificat.
Non quaero quae mea sunt. Non mea gratia sed Deus qui dedit hanc
sollicitudinem in corde meo, ut unus essem de venatoribus sive
piscatoribus quos olim Deus in novissimis diebus ante praenuntiavit.

12   Invidetur mihi. Quid faciam, Domine? Valde despicior. Ecce oves tuae
      circa me laniantur atque depraedantur, et supradictis latrunculis,
      iubente Corotico hostili mente. Longe est a caritate Dei traditor
      Christianorum in manus Scottorum atque Pictorum. Lupi rapaces
      deglutierunt gregem Domini, qui utique Hiberione cum summa
      diligentia optime crescebat, et filii Scottorum et filiae regulorum
      monachi et virgines Christi — enumerare nequeo. Quam ob rem
      iniuria iustorum non te placeat; etiam usque ad inferos non placebit.

13   Quis sanctorum non horreat iocundare vel convivium fruere cum
      talibus? De spoliis defunctorum Christianorum repleverunt domus
      suas, de rapinis vivunt. Nesciunt miseri, venenum letale cibum porri-
      gunt ad amicos et filios suos, sicut Eva non intellexit quod utique
      mortem tradidit viro suo. Sic sunt omnes qui male agunt; mortem
      perennem poenam operantur.

14   Consuetudo Romanorum Gallorum Christianorum; mittunt viros
      sanctos idoneos ad Francos et ceteras gentes cum tot milia solidorum
      ad redimendos captivos baptizatos. Tu potius interficis et vendis illos
      genti exterae ignoranti Deum; quasi in lupanar tradis membra Christi.
      Qualem spem habes in Deum, vel qui te consentit aut qui te commun-
      icat verbis adulationis? Deus iudicabit. Scriptum est enim: 'Non solum
      facientes mala sed etiam consentientes damnandi sunt.'

15   Nescio quid dicam vel quid loquar amplius de defunctis filiorum Dei,
      quos gladius supra modum dure tetigit. Scriptum est enim: 'Flete cum
      flentibus;' et iterum: 'Si dolet unum membrum, condoleant omnia
      membra.' Quapropter ecclesia plorat et plangit filios et filias suas quas
      adhuc gladius nondum interfecit, sed prolongati et exportati in longa
      terrarum, ubi peccatum manifeste graviter impudenter abundat; ibi
      venundati ingenui homines, Christiani in servitute redacti sunt,
      praesertim indignissimorum pessimorum apostatarumque Pictorum.

16   Idcirco cum tristitia et maerore vociferabo. O speciosissimi atque
      amantissimi fratres et filii quos in Christo genui (enumerare nequeo),
      quid faciam vobis? Non sum dignus Deo neque hominibus subvenire.
      Praevaluit iniquitas iniquorum super nos. Quasi extranei facti sumus.
      Forte non credunt unum baptismum percepimus vel unum Deum
      patrem habemus. Indignum est illis Hiberionaci* sumus. Sicut ait:
      'Nonne unum Deum habetis? Quid dereliquistis unusquisque proxim-
      um suum?'

17   Idcirco doleo pro vobis, doleo, carissimi mihi. Sed iterum gaudeo
      intra meipsum: non gratis laboravi vel peregrinatio mea in vacuum non
      fuit. Et contigit scelus tam horrendum ineffabile; Deo gratias, creduli

baptizati de saeculo recessistis ad paradisum. Cerno vos; migrare coepistis ubi nox non erit neque luctus neque mors amplius, sed exultabitis sicut vituli ex vinculis resoluti et conculcabitis iniquos et erunt cinis sub pedibus vestris.

18 Vos ergo regnabitis cum apostolis et prophetis atque martyribus. Aeterna regna capietis, sicut ipse testatur. Inquit: 'Venient ab oriente et occidente et recumbent cum Abraham et Isaac et Iacob in regno caelorum.' 'Foris canes et venefici et homicidae;' et: 'Mendacibus periuris pars eorum in stagnum ignis aeterni.' Non immerito ait apostolus: 'Ubi iustus vix salvus erit, peccator et impius transgressor legis ubi se recognoscet?'

19 Unde enim Coroticus cum suis sceleratissimis, rebellatores Christi, ubi se videbunt, qui mulierculas baptizatas praemia distribuunt, ob miserum regnum temporale quod utique in momento transeat? Sicut nubes vel fumus qui utique vento dispergitur, ita peccatores fraudulenti a facie Domini peribunt; iusti autem epulentur in magna constantia cum Christo, iudicabunt nationes et regibus iniquis dominabuntur in saecula saeculorum. Amen.

20 Testificor coram Deo et angelis suis quod ita erit sicut intimavit imperitiae meae. Non mea verba sed Dei et apostolorum atque prophetarum, quod ego Latinum exposui, qui nunquam enim mentiti sunt. 'Qui crediderit salvus erit, qui vero non crediderit condempnabitur;' Deus locutus est.

21 Quaeso plurimum ut quicumque famulus Dei promptus fuerit ut sit gerulus litterarum harum, ut nequaquam subtrahatur vel abscondatur a nemine, sed magis potius legatur coram cunctis plebibus et praesente ipso Corotico. Quod si Deus inspirat illos ut quandoque Deo resipiscant, ita ut vel sero paeniteant quod tam impie gesserunt (homicida erga fratres Domini!) et liberent captivas baptizatas quas ante ceperunt, ita ut mereantur Deo vivere et sani efficiantur hic et in aeternum! Pax Patri et Filio et Spiritui Sancto!

DICTA

1 Timorem Dei habui ducem iteneris mei per Gallias atque Italiam, etiam in insolis quae sunt in mari Terreno.

2 De saeculo requissistis ad paradissum. Deo gratias.

3 Aeclessia Scotorum immo Romanorum; ut Christiani ita ut Romani sitis ut decantetur vobiscum oportet omni hora orationis vox illa laudabilis Curie lession, Christe lession. Omnis aeclesia quae sequitur me cantet Cyrie lession, Christe lession; Deo gratias.

TEXTUAL NOTES

Confessio

1. ⟨filii Odissi⟩ *A* (*Marginal note*).
4. . didicimus *Bieler*: dicimus *DPCG*: diximus *RF*.
9. iura *J. Gwynn*: iure *MSS*.
10. imberbis *Ware*: inverbis (in verbis) *MSS*.
    ⟨non⟩ disertus *Stokes*: desertis (disertis *VRG*) *PFC*: de deeritis *D*. sermone ⟨m⟩ *White*.
13. dominicati *D*: domini (domni *PFCG*) ignari (gnari *P*) *PVRFCG*.
19. carne *G²*: carnes *PCG* (coxerunt carnes et comederunt ad satur- itatem *Probus*): canes *DVRF*.
24. peritissime *D*: -imi *P*: -imis *VCG*: perterritus *R*: apertissime *Bieler*.
29. ⟨scriptum quod⟩ *Bury*.
    quasi sibi se iunxisset *del. Grosjean*.
32. oriebatur *Bury*: orietur *MSS*.
34. tanta divinitate comparuisti *Bieler*: tantam divinitatem cooperuisti (cooperasti *P*) *PFCG*.
    adiuverit *Bieler*: audierit *MSS*.
35. idiotam *White*: ideo *MSS*.
42. et illae *Ware*: et (*om. P*) illas *MSS*: ex illis *Bieler*.
46. intellige *Grosjean*: intellegi *DPVC*: intelligi *G*:ᵇintellexi *F*.
49. ⟨non⟩ *Bieler*.
60 ⟨ipso⟩ *Bieler*: Domino *G*ˢˢ.

Epistola

2. atque Pictorum apostatarumque sanguilentos (sanguinolentos *G*) sanguinare *PFCG*: atque Pictorum apostatarum quasi sanguine volentes saginari *v* (. . . quasi anhelantes saginare *Grosjean*).
   innumerum numerum *Bury*: innumerum *FCG*: innumeros *v*: in numero *P*.
4. gehennae . . . se mancipabunt *Hitchcock*: gehenna . . . manci- pabuntur *Bieler*: gehennam (gehennae *G*) . . . mancipabunt *MSS*.
7. ⟨per⟩*Bieler*.
16. Hiberionaci *Bieler*: Hiberia nati *MSS*.

DECLARATION

1 I, Patrick, a sinner, quite uncultivated and the least of all the
faithful and utterly despicable to many, had as my father the
deacon Calpornius, son of the late Potitus, a priest, who
belonged to the town of Bannavem Taburniae; he had a small
estate nearby, and it was there that I was taken captive. I was
then about sixteen years old. I did not know the true God and I
was taken into captivity in Ireland with so many thousands; and
we deserved it, because we drew away from God and did not
keep His commandments and did not obey our priests who kept
reminding us of our salvation; and the Lord brought on us the
fury of His anger and scattered us among many peoples even
to the ends of the earth, where now I in my insignificance find
myself among foreigners.

2 And there the Lord opened up my awareness of my unbelief,
so that I might, however late, remember my faults and turn
with all my heart to the Lord my God, who had regard for my
lowly estate and took pity on my youth and ignorance and
watched over me before I knew Him and before I learned sense
or could distinguish between good and evil and who protected
me and comforted me as a father might his son.

3 And therefore I cannot keep silent — nor in fact would it be
proper to do so — about the great benefits and grace which the
Lord has deigned to confer on me in the land of my captivity;
because this is our way of giving thanks, after being chastised
by God and acknowledging Him to glorify and declare His
wonders before every nation under the whole of heaven.

4 For there is no other God, nor ever was before nor will be
hereafter except for God the Father, unbegotten, without
beginning, from whom is all beginning, possessing all things, as
we have learned; and His son Jesus Christ, whom we declare to
have existed always with the Father, before the beginning of
the world spiritually with the Father, begotten ineffably
before all beginning; and by Him were made things visible
and invisible; He was made man; He conquered death and was

received up into heaven to the Father; and He gave Him all power over every name of things in heaven and on earth and under the earth, that every tongue should confess to Him that Jesus Christ is Lord and God; in whom we believe, and we look to His imminent coming, as judge of the living and the dead, who will render to each one according to his deeds; and He poured out on us abundantly His Holy Spirit, the gift and pledge of immortality, who makes those who believe and obey to be sons of God and heirs along with Christ; Him we confess and worship as one God in the Trinity of sacred name.

5   For He Himself said through His prophet: 'Call on Me in the day of your distress, and I shall deliver you and you will glorify Me.' (Psalms 49.15)   And again He says: 'It is honourable to declare and proclaim the works of God.' (Tobit 12.7)

6   Though I am imperfect in many respects, I wish my brothers and kinsfolk to know what sort of man I am, so that they may be able to conceive of my soul's desire.

7   I am well aware of the affirmation of my Lord, who declares in the psalm: 'You shall destroy those who speak a lie.' (Psalms 5.7) And again He says: 'The lying mouth kills the soul.' (Wisdom 1.11)   And likewise the Lord says in the gospel: 'As for the idle word which men speak, they shall give account for it in the day of judgement.' (Matthew 12.36)

8   And therefore I ought to dread with great fear and trembling this sentence on that day when no-one will be able to steal away or hide, but we shall all, yes all, have to give account for even the smallest of our sins before the judgement-seat of Christ the Lord.

9   Therefore I have long had it in mind to write but have in fact hesitated up till now, for I was afraid to expose myself to the criticism of men's tongues, because I have not studied like others, who have successfully imbibed both law and Holy Scripture alike and have never changed their language from infancy but rather have always been bringing it nearer to perfection. For my words and style have been translated into a foreign language; that, and how I was taught and educated to express myself, can easily be gathered from the flavour of my writing, because, it is written, 'The wise man will be recognised by his speech, and so too will understanding and knowledge and the teaching of truth.' (Ecclesiasticus 4.29)

10   But what is the point of excuses, however truthful, especially when
      linked with my audacity in aspiring now, in my old age, to what I did
      not acquire in my youth? For my sins prevented me from consolidat-
      ing what I had previously read through. But who believes me even if I
      repeat what I have said before? As a youth, indeed almost a boy
      without any beard, I was taken captive, before I knew what to desire
      and what I ought to avoid. And so, then, today I am ashamed and
      terrified to expose my awkwardness, because, being inarticulate, I am
      unable to explain briefly what I mean, as my mind and spirit long and
      the inclination of my heart indicates.

11   But if I had in fact had the same privileges as others, out of gratitude I
      should not keep silent, and if by chance certain people feel that I am
      pushing myself forward in this for all my ignorance and slow tongue,
      it is, after all, written; 'The stammering tongues shall quickly learn to
      speak peace.' (Isaiah 32.4)   How much more ought we to make that
      our aim, since we are, as it is written, 'The letter of Christ for salvat-
      ion to the ends of the earth,' and even if it is not eloquent, †.........†
      'It has been written in your hearts not with ink but with the Spirit of
      the living God.' (2 Corinthians 3.2—3)   And again the Spirit declares
      that rusticity too was created by the Most High. (Ecclesiasticus 7.16)

12   And so I am in the first place countrified, an exile, yes, unlearned, with
      no idea of how to look to the future; but this I know for certain, that
      in fact before I was humbled I was like a stone lying in deep mud; and
      He that is mighty came and in His mercy lifted me up and indeed
      raised me up and placed me on the top of the wall; and so I ought to
      shout out aloud to render some thanks to the Lord for His great
      benefits here and for ever, benefits which the human mind cannot
      assess.

13   So then, be amazed, you great and small that fear God, and you clerical
      intellectuals, listen and take stock. Who raised me up, a fool,from the
      midst of those who seem to be wise and learned in the law and power-
      ful in speaking and all else, and inspired me in preference to others,
      execrated as I am by this world, to prove fit to help (if only I could!),
      faithfully, with fear and reverence and without complaint, the people
      to which the love of Christ brought and gave me for the rest of my life,
      if I am worthy; in short, to serve them sincerely and with humility?

14   And so in accordance with the measure of one's faith in the Trinity
      one ought to be explicit and to make known God's gift and His
      everlasting consolation without jibbing at the danger, and to spread
      God's name everywhere confidently and fearlessly, so that even after
      my death I may leave a legacy to my brethren and sons whom I

baptised in so many thousands in the Lord.

15   And I was not worthy nor such that the Lord should grant His
      humble servant this, should, after such trials and hardships, after
      captivity and a long period of years, give me such grace in regard to
      that people — something which I never hoped for nor imagined in
      the days of my youth.

16   But after I reached Ireland, well, I pastured the flocks every day and
      I used to pray many times a day; more and more did my love of God
      and my fear of Him increase, and my faith grew and my spirit was
      stirred, and as a result I would say up to a hundred prayers in one
      day, and almost as many at night; I would even stay in the forests and
      on the mountain and would wake to pray before dawn in all weathers,
      snow, frost, rain; and I felt no harm and there was no listlessness in me
      — as I now realise, it was because the Spirit was fervent within me.

17   And it was in fact there that one night while asleep I heard a voice
      saying to me: 'You do well to fast, since you will soon be going to
      your home country;' and again, very shortly after, I heard this
      prophecy: 'See, your ship is ready.' And it was not near at hand but
      was perhaps two hundred miles away, and I had never been there and
      did not know a living soul there. And then I soon ran away and
      abandoned the man with whom I had been for six years, and I came
      in God's strength, for He granted me a successful journey and I had
      nothing to fear, till I reached that ship.

18   Now on the very day that I arrived the ship was launched, and I said
      that I had the wherewithal for my passage with them; and as for the
      captain, he was not pleased and replied sharply and with annoyance:
      'You will be wasting your time asking to go with us.' On hearing this
      I left them to go to the hut where I was staying, and on the way I
      began to pray and before I had finished my prayer I heard one of
      them; he was shouting loudly after me: 'Come quickly, they are
      calling you.' And immediately I returned to them and they proceeded
      to say to me: 'Come, we are taking you on trust; make friends with
      us in whatever way you wish' (and so that day I refused to suck their
      nipples because of the fear of God; however, I had hopes of their
      coming to faith in Jesus Christ, because they were pagans), and as a
      result I got a place with them, and we set sail at once.

19   Three days later we made land and we travelled through a wilderness
      for twenty-eight days, and they ran out of food and hunger overtook
      them, and the next day the captain approached me and said: 'What
      about it, Christian? You say your god is great and all-powerful; well

then, why can you not pray for us? We are in danger of starving; there is little chance of our ever seeing a living soul.' I told them confidently: 'Turn trustingly and with all your heart to the Lord my God — because nothing is impossible for Him; and this day He will send you food for your journey until you are fully satisfied; for He has an abundance everywhere.' And with God's help it turned out so; lo and behold, a herd of pigs appeared in the way before our eyes, and they killed many of them and stayed there for two nights and fully recovered and had their fill of the pigs' meat, for many of them had collapsed and been left half-dead by the wayside; and after this they gave grateful thanks to God, and I gained great respect in their eyes, and from that day they had plenty of food. They even found some wild honey and offered me a piece; and one of them said: 'It is a sacrifice.' Thanks be to God, I tasted none of it.

20 Now that same night I was asleep, and Satan attacked me violently, something which I shall remember as long as I am in this body; and there fell on top of me a huge rock, as it were, and I was completely paralysed. But what gave me, in my spiritual ignorance, the idea of calling on Helias? And meanwhile I saw the sun rising in the sky and on shouting 'Helias, Helias' with all my might, see, the brilliance of that sun fell on me and at once shook me free of all the weight; and I believe that I was aided by Christ my Lord and that His Spirit was already crying out for me, and I hope that it will be so in the day of my affliction, as He says in the gospel: 'In that day,' the Lord declares, 'it is not you who speak but the Spirit of your Father who speaks within you.' (Matthew 10.19-20)

21 (And after many years I was once again taken captive. And so on that first night I stayed with my captors. And I heard a divine voice prophesying to me: 'You will be with them for two months.' And so it came about; sixty nights later the Lord delivered me from their hands.)

22 Now as we travelled He provided us with food and fire and dry weather every day until on the tenth day we reached human habitation; as I indicated above, we had travelled for twenty-eight days through the wilderness and on the night that we reached human habitation we had in fact no food left.

23 And again a few years later I was in Britain with my kinsfolk, and they welcomed me as a son and asked me earnestly not to go off anywhere and leave them this time, after the great tribulations which I had been through. And it was there that I saw one night in a vision a man coming as it were from Ireland (his name was Victoricus), with

countless letters, and he gave me one of them, and I read the heading of the letter, 'The Voice of the Irish.' and as I read these opening words aloud, I imagined at that very instant that I heard the voice of those who were beside the forest of Foclut which is near the western sea; and thus they cried, as though with one voice: 'We beg you, holy boy, to come and walk again among us;' and I was stung with remorse in my heart and could not read on, and so I awoke. Thanks be to God, that after so many years the Lord bestowed on them according to their cry.

24 And another night (I do not know, God knows, whether it was within me or beside me) I was addressed in words †......† which I heard and yet could not understand, except that at the end of the prayer He spoke thus: 'He who gave His life for you, He it is who speaks within you,' and so I awoke, overjoyed.

25 And again I saw Him praying within me and I was, as it were, inside my own body and I heard Him above me, that is to say above my inner self, and He was praying there powerfully and groaning; and meanwhile I was dumbfounded and astonished and wondered who it could be that was praying within me, but at the end of the prayer He spoke and said that He was the Spirit, and so I awoke and remembered the apostle's words: 'The Spirit helps the weaknesses of our prayer; for we do not know what to pray for as we ought; but the Spirit Himself intercedes for us with unspeakable groans which cannot be expressed in words;' (Romans 8.26) and again:'The Lord our advocate intercedes for us.' (cf. 1 John 2.1)

26 And when I was attacked by a number of my elders, who came and brought up my sins against my arduous episcopate, certainly that day I was struck a heavy blow so that I might fall here and for ever; but the Lord graciously spared me, who was a stranger in a foreign land for His name's sake, and He helped me greatly when I was trampled under foot in this way. I pray God that it may not be reckoned to them as a sin that I well and truly fell into disgrace and scandal.

27 After thirty years they found a pretext for their allegations against me in a confession which I had made before I was a deacon. In a depressed and worried state of mind I mentioned to a close friend what I had done as a boy one day, indeed in the space of one hour, because I was not yet proof against temptation. I do not know, God knows, whether I was fifteen years old at the time, and I did not believe in the living God, nor had I done since earliest childhood; but I remained in death and unbelief till I was severely chastened and in truth humiliated by hunger and nakedness, and every day too.

28 On the other hand I did not go to Ireland of my own accord, until I was nearly at the end of my strength; but this was really rather to my own good, since as a result I was reformed by the Lord, and He fitted me to be today what was once far from me, that I should be concerned and busily active for the salvation of others, whereas at that time I took no thought even for myself.

29 Therefore on the day on which I was rejected by the aforesaid and abovementioned, that same night I saw in a vision a document opposite my face, without honour, and meanwhile I heard a divine prophecy saying to me: 'We were grieved to see the face of our elect with his name stripped of all honour;' and He did not say: 'You were grieved to see,' but 'We were grieved to see,' [as though He included Himself with him], just as He said: 'He that touches you is as he that touches the apple of My eye.' (Zechariah 2.8)

30 And so I give thanks to Him who strengthened me in all things, so as not to hinder me from setting out on the journey on which I had decided and also from my work which I had learned from Christ my Lord, but rather I felt within me considerable strength as a result, and my faith was proved before God and man.

31 And so I say boldly, my conscience does not reproach me here or hereafter. God is my witness that I have not lied in my account to you.

32 But rather I feel sorry for my close friend, that we deserved to hear such a prophecy as this. A man to whom I have entrusted my very soul! And I learned from a number of the brethren before that defence of my case (at which I was not present, not was I in Britain, nor did I initiate it) that he would take up the cudgels for me: he had even told me himself from his own mouth: 'See, you should be raised to the rank of bishop' — which I did not deserve. But how did he take it into his head afterwards, publicly, before everyone, good and evil, to discredit me for something which he had previously been glad to pardon of his own accord, as had the Lord too, who is greater than all?

33 Enough said. But still, I ought not to conceal God's gift which He lavished on us in the land of my captivity, because then I sought Him earnestly and I found Him there, and He protected me from all evils, as I believe, because of His Spirit dwelling in me, which has been at work within me up to the present day. Another bold statement; but God knows, if it were a man who had told me this, perhaps I would have kept silent for the love of Christ.

34 And so I give untiring thanks to my God who kept me faithful in the

day of my temptation, so that today I may confidently make an offering to Him of my soul as a living sacrifice to Christ my Lord, who protected me from all my afflictions, so that I may also say: who am I, Lord, or what is my calling, that You appeared to me in such divine power, so that today among the heathen I might steadfastly exalt and magnify Your name wherever I find myself, and not only in success but also in affliction? And so whatever happens to me, be it good or bad, I should accept it calmly and always give thanks to God who showed me that I might place implicit and unlimited trust in Him, and who helped me so that I, for all my ignorance, should in the last days venture to undertake such devout and wonderful work, so that I should follow to some extent the example of those who the Lord long ago foretold would proclaim His gospel as a testimony to all the nations before the end of the world — and so we have seen and so it has been fulfilled. Look, we are witnesses that the gospel has been preached to the point beyond which there is no-one.

35 But it would be tedious to relate all my labours in detail or even partially. I shall briefly tell how God in His great mercy on many occasions freed me from slavery and from the twelve dangers in which my life was threatened, quite apart from many traps and things which I cannot put into words. I should not like to cause offence to my readers; but God is my witness, who knows all things even before they h pen, that He frequently gave me a warning in a divine prophecy, despite my being a poor waif and uneducated.

36 From where did this vision come to me? It was not within me, who neither knew the number of my days nor had any knowledge of God. From where did that gift, so great and so salutary, afterwards come, the gift of knowing and loving God, but at the cost of losing family and homeland?

37 And I was offered many gifts, with weeping and tears, and I offended them, and I also acted against the wishes of a number of my elders, but under God's guidance I refused to agree or defer to them; not that it was my grace, it was God, who is victorious in me and withstands them all, when I came to the peoples of Ireland to preach the gospel and endure insults from unbelievers; and to hear criticism of my travels; and to endure many persecutions, even to the extent of being put in prison, and to give my freedom for the benefit of others, and, if I so deserve, I am ready to give even my life without delay and joyfully for His name; and I wish to expend it there even to the point of death, if God would so grant me.

38 because I am very much God's debtor; for He granted me such grace

48

that through me many peoples should be reborn in God and afterwards
be confirmed and that clergy should everywhere be ordained for them,
to serve a people just now coming to the faith, and which the Lord
chose from the ends of the earth, as He had promised of old through His
prophets: 'The nations will come to you from the ends of the earth and
will say: "How false the idols are which our fathers made for themselves; they are quite useless;" ' (Jeremiah 16.19) and again: 'I have
put you as a light among the nations, to be a means of salvation to the
ends of the earth.' (Acts 13.47)

39 And I wish to wait there for His promise (and He of course never
deceives), as He promises in the gospel: 'They shall come from the east
and from the west and shall sit down at table with Abraham and Isaac
and Jacob,' (Matthew 8.11) as we believe that believers will surely come
from the whole world.

40 And so then, it is our duty to fish well and diligently, as the Lord
urges and teaches us, saying: 'Follow me, and I shall make you become
fishers of men;' (Matthew 4.19) and again He says through the prophets:
'See, I send many fishers and hunters, says God;' (Jeremiah 16.16)
etc...... And so it was our bounden duty to spread our nets, so that a
vast multitude and throng might be caught for God and there might be
clergy everywhere to baptise and exhort a people that was poor and
needy, as the Lord says — He urges and teaches in the gospel, saying:
'So go now, teach all nations, baptising them in the name of the Father
and of the Son and of the Holy Spirit, teaching them to observe all
that I have commanded you; and see, I am with you every single day
right to the end of the world;' (Matthew 28. 19-20) and again He
says: 'Go therefore into the whole world and preach the gospel to
every creature; he that believes and is baptised shall be saved; but he
that does not believe shall be damned;' (Mark 16.15-16) and again:
'This gospel of the kingdom shall be preached throughout the whole
world as a testimony to all nations; and then the end shall come.'
(Matthew 24.14) And likewise the Lord foretells through the prophet,
saying: 'And it will be in the last days, says the Lord, I shall pour out
of My spirit upon all flesh, and your sons and daughters will prophesy
and your young men will see visions and your old men dream dreams,
and indeed in those days I shall pour out of My spirit upon My servants
and My maidservants and they will prophesy;' (Acts 2.17-18; cf. Joel
2.28-29) and in Hosea He says: 'A people that is not Mine I shall call
My people, and a people that has not obtained mercy I shall call one
that has obtained mercy. And it shall be in the place where it was said:
"You are not My people" — in that place they will be called the sons
of the living God.' (Romans 9.25-26; cf. Hosea 1.9-10)

41 And how has it lately come about in Ireland that those who never had
    any knowledge of God but up till now always worshipped idols and
    abominations are now called the people of the Lord and the sons of
    God, and sons and daughters of Irish underkings are seen to be monks
    and virgins of Christ?

42 And there was also a blessed lady of native Irish birth and high rank,
    very beautiful and grown up, whom I baptised; and a few days later
    she found some reason to come to us and indicated that she had
    received a message from an angel of God, and the angel had urged her
    too to become a virgin of Christ and to draw near to God. Thanks
    be to God, six days later she most commendably and enthusiastically
    took up that same course that all virgins of God also do — not with
    their fathers' consent; no, they endure persecution and their own
    parents' unfair reproaches, and yet their number grows larger and
    larger (and we do not know the numbers of our family of faith who
    have been reborn there), not to mention widows and the self-denying.
    But it is the women kept in slavery who suffer especially; they even
    have to endure constant threats and terrorisation; but the Lord has
    given grace to many of His handmaidens, for though they are forbidden
    to do so, they resolutely follow His example.

43 And so even if I wanted to part with them and head for Britain — and
    I would have been only too glad to do so, to see my homeland and
    family; and not only that, but to go on to Gaul to visit the brethren
    and to see the face of my Lord's holy men; God knows that I longed
    to, but I am bound by the Spirit who testifies to me that if I do so He
    will mark me out as guilty, and I am afraid of wasting the labour which
    I have begun — and not I, but Christ the Lord who commanded me
    to come to be with them for the rest of my life, if the Lord so desire
    and shield me from every evil way, so that I may not sin before Him.

44 Now I hope that I did what was right, but I do not trust myself for as
    long as I am in this mortal body, because he is strong who strives daily
    to turn me away from the faith and from the purity of true religion
    to which I aspire to the end of my life for Christ my Lord; but the
    hostile flesh is always dragging me down to death, in other words to
    indulgence in illicit temptations; and I know in part why I have not led
    a perfect life like other believers, but I declare it to my Lord and do
    not blush in His sight, because I am not lying; since I came to know
    Him, from my youth the love of God and fear of Him have grown in
    me, and up till now, by God's favour, I have kept the faith.

45 He who wants to can laugh and jeer, but I shall not keep silent nor
    keep hidden the signs and wonders which have been shown me by the

Lord many years before they took place, as He knows all things, even before the world began.

46 And so I ought to give thanks to God without ceasing; for He often forgave my stupidity, my carelessness, and in more than one instance, so as not to be extremely angry with me, who have been assigned as His helper although I was not quick to give my assent as had been revealed to me and as the Spirit kept prompting; and the Lord took pity on me thousands and thousands of times, because He saw in me that I was ready but that I did not know what to do in my position; for many tried to prevent this mission and talked among themselves behind my back and said: 'Why is this fellow walking into danger among enemies who do not know God?' Not that they were being malicious, but they did not like the idea, as I can myself confirm — take it from me, it was because of my lack of education; and I was not quick to recognise the grace which was then in me; now I appreciate that I should have done so before.

47 So now I have given an indication in plain terms to my brethren and fellow-servants of Christ who have believed me because of what I have said before and now foretell to strengthen and reinforce your faith. If only you too would make greater efforts and do better. This will be my pride and joy, because 'a wise son is his father's pride.' (Proverbs 10.1)

48 You know, and so does God, how I have lived among you from my youth in the faith of truth and in sincerity of heart. As for the heathen amongst whom I live, I have always been honest in my dealings with them and always shall be. God knows I have cheated none of them, nor would I think of it, for God and His church's sake, in case of stirring up persecution against them and all of us and in case the Lord's name should be blasphemed because of me; for it is written: 'Woe to the man through whom the name of the Lord is blasphemed.' (Matthew 18.7)

49 For though I am entirely untalented, I have done my best to safeguard myself, even in my dealings with Christian brethren and virgins of Christ and with pious women, who would give me unsolicited gifts and throw some of their jewellery on the altar, and I would return it to them, and they would take offence at my doing so; but I did so for the hope of eternity, to safeguard myself carefully in everything so that they would not catch me out or the ministry of my service under some pretext of my dishonesty and so that I would not give unbelievers the slightest opportunity for denigration or disparagement.

50 But perhaps when I baptised so many thousands I hoped for even a halfpenny from any of them? Tell me, and I will give it back. Or when the Lord everywhere ordained clergy through someone as ordinary as me and I conferred on each of them his function free, if I asked any of them for even so much as the price of my shoe, tell it against me, and I shall give it back to you.

51 No, rather I spent money on your behalf so that they would accept me, and I travelled amongst you and everywhere for your sake, beset by many dangers, even to the remote districts beyond which there was no-one and where no-one had ever penetrated to baptise or ordain clergy or confirm the people. With God's favour I have produced all these results tirelessly and most gladly for your salvation.

52 From time to time I gave presents to the kings, quite apart from the payments I made to their sons who travel with me; however, they arrested me and my companions and that day were extremely eager to kill me, but my time had not yet come; they seized everything that they found on us and put me in irons; and fourteen days later the Lord released me from their power, and we had restored to us all our belongings for God's sake and the sake of the close friends whom we previously acquired.

53 But you know from experience how much I have paid to those who adminstered justice in all the districts, whom I was in the habit of visiting. I reckon that I must have dispensed to them the price of fifteen men at the least, so that you may enjoy me and I always enjoy you in God. I have no regrets; indeed I am not satisfied with that — I still spend and I will spend more. The Lord has it in His power to grant me afterwards that I may spend myself for your souls.

54 See, I call God as my witness upon my soul that I am not lying; nor would I have thought of writing to you to afford an opportunity for flattery or covetousness, nor is it that I hope for honour from any of you. Sufficient is the honour which is not yet seen but of which the heart is assured; and He that has made the promise is faithful, He never lies.

55 But I see that even in the present world I have been exalted beyond measure by the Lord, and I did not deserve or merit that He should grant me this, since I am only too well aware that I am better suited to poverty and adversity than riches and luxury (but Christ the Lord too was poor for our sakes, and I am hapless and unfortunate and do not have any wealth now, even if I wanted it), nor is this just my personal opinion of myself, because every day I expect to be killed, betrayed,

reduced to slavery, or whatever; but I fear none of these, because of the promises of Heaven; for I have cast myself into the hands of Almighty God, who reigns everywhere; as the prophet says: 'Cast your cares upon the Lord and He will sustain you.' (Psalm 54.23)

56 See now I commend my soul to my God in whom we trust absolutely, for whom I am an ambassador despite my obscurity, because He is no respecter of persons and He chose me for this task, to be just one among the least of His servants.

57 And so I shall give thanks to Him for all His benefits to me. But what shall I say, what shall I promise to my Lord, for I can do nothing unless He grant me it? But let Him search my heart and inmost soul; for I am eager, yes, exceedingly eager, and I was ready for Him to grant me to drink of His cup, as He bestowed it also on His other loving followers.

58 And so may God never allow me to be separated from His people which He has won in the ends of the earth. I pray to God to give me perseverance and to deign to grant that I prove a faithful witness to Him until I pass on, for my God's sake.

59 And if I have ever aimed at any good for my God's sake, whom I love, I beg Him to grant that I may shed my blood for His name along with those exiles and captives, though I should even go without burial or my body be torn most pitiably limb from limb for dogs or savage beasts to share or the birds of the air devour it. It is my strong conviction that if this should happen to me, I would have gained my soul as well as my body; for beyond any doubt in that day we shall rise in the sun's brilliant light, that is, in the glory of Christ Jesus our redeemer, to be sons of the living God and heirs with Christ and shaped to His like-ness; for we shall reign from Him and through Him and in Him.

60 For this sun which we see rises daily for us at His command, but it will never reign nor its splendour endure; no, all that worship it shall be doomed to dreadful punishment. But we who believe in and worship the true Sun, Christ, who will never perish — nor will anyone who has done His will but he will abide for ever just as Christ abides for ever, who reigns with God the Father Almighty and with the Holy Spirit before the world began and now and for ever and ever, Amen.

61 See, over and over again I shall briefly set out the words of my declaration. I attest in truth and exultation of heart before God and His holy angels that I never had any cause, except His gospel and His promises, ever to return to that people from which I had previously

escaped with such difficulty.

62 But I beg those who believe in and fear God, whoever deigns to look at or receive this document which the unlearned sinner Patrick drew up in Ireland, that no-one should ever say that if I have achieved anything, however trivial, or may have shown the way according to God's good pleasure, it was my ignorance at work, but consider and accept as the undeniable truth that it would have been God's gift. And this is my declaration before I die.

LETTER

1   I, Patrick, a sinner, yes, and unlearned, established in Ireland, put on record that I am bishop. I am strongly convinced that what I am I have received from God. And so I live among barbarian peoples, a stranger and an exile for the love of God; He is my witness if it is so. Not that I wanted to utter anything from my lips so harshly and bluntly, but I am compelled by my zeal for God, and Christ's truth has roused me to do so, for the love of my neighbour and my children, for whose sakes I gave up homeland and family and my life even to the point of death. If I so deserve, I live for my God, to teach the heathen, even if I am despised by some.

2   With my own hand I have written and composed these words to be given, delivered and sent to the soldiers of Coroticus — I do not say to my fellow-citizens nor to fellow-citizens of the holy Romans, but to fellow-citizens of the demons, because of their evil actions. Like the enemy they live in death, as allies of Irish and of Picts and apostates. These blood-thirsty men are bloody with the blood of innocent Christians, whom I have begotten for God in countless numbers and have confirmed in Christ!

3   On the day after the neophytes, clothed in white, had received the chrism (its fragrance was on their brows as they were butchered and put to the sword by those I have mentioned), I sent a letter with a holy priest whom I had taught from early childhood, and he was accompanied by some clerics; the letter requested that they should grant us some of the booty and baptised prisoners that they had captured; they roared with laughter at them.

4   And so I do not know what to lament more, those who were killed or those they took prisoner or those whom Satan has sorely ensnared. They shall be delivered up to hell along with him in eternal punishment because undoubtedly he who commits a sin is a slave and is called the son of Satan.

5   Therefore let every man who fears God acknowledge that they are estranged from me and from Christ my God, for whom I am an ambassador; the man is a patricide, a fratricide, they are ravening

wolves, devouring God's people like so much bread, as is said: 'The wicked have destroyed Your Law, O Lord,' (Psalms 118.126) which in these last times He had most graciously planted in Ireland and which had become established with God's favour.

6   I am not claiming more than my due; I have a share with those whom He called and predestined to preach the gospel right to the ends of the earth in the midst of no small persecution, even if the enemy shows his resentment through the unjust rule of Coroticus, who does not fear God or His priests whom He has chosen and endowed with the supreme, divine and exalted power that those whom they bound on earth should be bound in heaven also.

7   And therefore I make this earnest appeal to all you men of piety and humble heart; it is not right to curry favour with such as these nor to take food or drink with them, nor ought one to accept their alms, until they make amends to God by gruelling penance, with shedding of tears, and free God's servants and the baptised handmaids of Christ, for whom He died and was crucified.

8   'The Most High rejects the gifts of the wicked. He who offers sacrifice from the goods of the poor is like the man who sacrifices the son before his father's eyes.' (Ecclesiasticus 34.23-24) 'The wealth,' it is written, 'which he has amassed unjustly will be vomited from out of his belly; the angel of death drags him away; he will be tormented by the wrath of dragons; the serpent's tongue will kill him, and unquenchable fire devours him.' (Job 20.15ff) And so, 'Woe to those who fill themselves with what is not theirs;' (Habakkuk 2.6) or, 'What does it profit a man to gain the whole world and suffer the loss of his own soul?' (Matthew 16.26)

9   It would be tedious to deal with each individual point, to make declarations and to collect texts on such greed from the whole Law. Avarice is a mortal sin. 'Thou shalt not covet thy neighbour's property. Thou shalt not kill.' (Exodus 20.17,13) A murderer cannot be with Christ. 'He who hates his brother is reckoned a murderer;' (1 John 3.15) or, 'He who does not love his brother dwells in death.' (1 John 3.14) How much more guilty is he who has sullied his hands with the blood of the sons of God, whom He recently won in the ends of the earth thanks to the exhortation of one as insignificant as I am!

10   Did I come to Ireland without God's favour or according to the flesh? Who forced me? I am obliged by the Spirit not to see any of my kinsfolk. Does it come from me that I show devout mercy towards the

very people which once took me captive and harried the slaves of my
father's house, male and female? I was free-born according to the flesh;
my father was a decurion. I sold my good birth (not that I am ashamed
or regret it) in the interest of others. In short, I am a slave in Christ to
a foreign people for the ineffable glory of the everlasting life which is
in Christ Jesus our Lord.

11 And if my own people do not recognise me, well, a prophet does not
have honour in his own country. Perhaps we are not of one fold and do
not have one God as father, as Christ says: 'He who is not with Me is
against Me, and he who does not gather with Me scatters.' (Matthew
12.30) We are at cross purposes; one destroys, another builds. I am
not seeking what is my own. It is not my grace but God who laid this
responsibility in my heart, to be one of His hunters or fishers whom
God once foretold would appear in the last days.

12 I am resented. What should I do, Lord? I am very much despised. See,
Your sheep are torn to pieces around me and are carried off, and by
the raiders I have mentioned, on the aggressive orders of Coroticus. Far
from God's love is the man who delivers Christians into the hands of
Irish and Picts. Ravening wolves have devoured the Lord's flock, which
was in fact increasing excellently and most actively, and sons of the
Irish and daughters of their underkings were monks and virgins of
Christ — I cannot count their number. Therefore be not pleased at the
wrong done to the righteous; even as far as hell it shall not be pleasing.

13 Which of the saints would not shudder at the thought of making merry
or feasting with such men? They have filled their homes with spoils
taken from dead Christians, they live by plunder. The wretches do not
realise it, they are offering deadly poison as food to their friends and
children, just as Eve did not realise that she in fact handed death to
her husband. All who do evil are so; they bring death on themselves
as their eternal punishment.

14 Here is the custom of the Roman Christians in Gaul; they send suitable holy men to the Franks and other peoples with so many thousand
solidi to ransom baptised captives; whereas you kill them or sell them
to a foreign people which does not know God; you commit the
members of Christ as though to a brothel. What hope do you have in
God, or indeed anyone who agrees with you or converses with you in
words of flattery? God will judge; for it is written: 'Not only those who
do evil but also those who agree with them are to be damned.' (Romans
1.32)

15 I do not know what more to say or speak concerning those of the sons

of God who have departed, whom the sword struck all too hard.
For it is written: 'Weep with those that weep;' (*Romans 12.15*)
and again, 'If one member grieves, let all the members share that
grief.' (1 *Corinthians 12.26*) Therefore the church mourns and weeps
for its sons and daughters who so far have not been put to the sword,
but have been carried far off and transported to distant lands, where
sin is rife, openly, grievously and shamelessly; and there freeborn
men have been sold, Christians reduced to slavery - and what is more,
as slaves of the utterly iniquitous, evil and apostate Picts.

16   Therefore I shall lift up my voice in grief and sorrow. You most
radiant and beloved brothers and children whom I have begotten in
Christ (I cannot count your number), what can I do for you? I am not
worthy to help God or man. The wickedness of the wicked has prevailed over us. We have become like outsiders. Perhaps they do not
believe we have received one baptism or have one God as Father. It is
an affront to them that we are Irish. As is written: 'Have you not one
God? Why have you one and all abandoned your neighbour?'
(*Malachia 2.10*).

17   Therefore I grieve for you, I grieve, my dearly beloved friends. Yet
there again, I rejoice within myself; I have not laboured for nothing
and my travels have not been in vain. And yet such an unspeakably
horrible crime took place; but thank God, it was as baptised believers
that you departed from this world to go to Paradise. I can see you;
you have begun your journey to where there will be no night nor
mourning nor death any more, but you will leap for joy like calves
freed of their bonds and will trample on the wicked, and they will be
ashes under your feet.

18   And so you will reign with the apostles and prophets and martyrs.
You will gain the eternal realms, just as He bears witness, saying; 'They
shall come from the East and from the West and shall lie down with
Abraham and Isaac and Jacob in the kingdom of heaven.'
(*Matthew 8.11*) 'Outside are dogs and sorcerers and murderers;'
(*Revelation 22.15*) and, 'As for lying oath-breakers, their lot will be
in the lake of everlasting fire.' (*Revelation 21.8*) Not without cause
does the apostle say: 'When the just shall scarcely be saved, where will
the sinner and ungodly transgressor of the Law find himself?' (1 *Peter
4.18*).

19   So then, what of Coroticus and his villains, these rebels against Christ,
where will they see themselves, they who allot poor baptised women
as prizes, for the sake of a miserable temporal kingdom which will in

any case pass away in a moment? Like clouds or smoke which is soon scattered by the wind, so deceitful sinners shall perish from before the Lord's face; but the righteous shall feast in full assurance with Christ; they shall judge the nations and hold sway over wicked kings for ever and ever, Amen.

20   I testify before God and His angels that it will be just as He has indicated to me in my ignorance. These are not my words but those of God and His apostles and prophets, which I have set out in Latin - and they have never lied. 'He who believes will be saved, but he who does not believe will be damned;' (*Mark 16.16*) God has spoken.

21   I earnestly beg that whichever servant of God is ready and willing should be the bearer of this letter, so that it may not be suppressed or hidden on any account by anyone, but rather be read out in front of all the people and in the presence of Coroticus himself. But if only God may inspire them to come to their senses eventually and return to God, so that, however late, they repent of acting so sacreligiously (murderer that he is of the Lord's brethren!) and free the baptised women whom they previously took captive, so that they may be found worthy to live for God and may be made whole here and for ever! Peace to Father, Son and Holy Ghost. Amen.

SAYINGS

1. I had the fear of God as my guide for my journey through Gaul and Italy, and also on the islands in the Tyrrhenian sea.

2. You have departed from this world to go to Paradise. Thanks be to God.

3. The church of the Irish, or rather of the Romans; in order to be Christians like the Romans, you should chant among yourselves at every hour of prayer that praiseworthy cry, *Kyrie eleison, Christe eleison.* Let every church which follows me chant *Kyrie eleison, Christe eleison;* Thanks be to God.

VITA

Preface

Quoniam quidem, mi domine Aido, multi conati sunt ordinare narrationem utique istam secundum quod patres eorum et qui ministri ab initio fuerunt sermonis tradiderunt illis, sed propter difficillimum narrationis opus diversasque opiniones et plurimorum plurimas suspiciones nunquam ad unum certumque historiae tramitem pervenierunt; ideo, ni fallor, iuxta hoc nostrorum proverbium, ut deducuntur pueri in ambiteathrum, in hoc periculossum et profundum narrationis sanctae pylagus, turgentibus proterve gurgitum aggeribus, inter acutissimos carubdes per ignota aequora insitos, a nullis adhuc lintribus, excepto tantum uno patris mei Coguitosi, * expertum atque occupatum, ingenioli mei puerilem remi cymbam deduxi. Sed ne magnum de parvo videar finguere, pauca haec de multis sancti Patricii gestis parva peritia, incertis auctoribus, memoria labili, attrito sensu, vili sermone, sed affectu piissimo caritatis, sanctitatis tuae et auctoritatis imperio oboediens, carptim gravatimque explicare aggrediar.

1 De ortu Patricii et eius prima captivitate.
2 De navigio eius cum gentibus et vexatione diserti et cibo sibi et gentilibus divinitus delato.
3 De secunda captura, quam senis decies diebus ab inimicis pertulerat.
4 De susceptione sua a parentibus ubi agnoverunt eum.
5 De aetate eius quando iens videre sedem apostolicam voluit discere sapientiam.
6 De inventione sancti Germani in Galliis, et ideo non exivit ultra.
7 De aetate eius quando vissitavit eum anguelus ut veniret adhuc.
8 De reversione eius de Gallis et ordinatione Palladii et mox morte eius.
9 De ordinatione eius ab Amathorege episcopo, defuncto Palladio.
10 De rege gentili †habeto† in Temoria quando venerat sanctus Patricius babtismum portans.
11 De primo eius itenere in hac insola ut seipsum redemeret o Miliucc priusquam alios a demonio traheret.
12 De morte Milcon et verbo Patricii de semine eius.
13 De consilio sancti Patricii ubi hessitum est de celebratione primi paschae.

14 De oblatione primo pasca in hac insola facta.
15 De festivitate gentili in Temoria eadem nocte qua sanctus Patricius pasca adoravit.
16 De gressu regis Loiguri de Temoria ad Patricium in nocte paschae.
17 De vocatione Patricii ad regem et fide Eirc filii Dego et morte magi in illa nocte.
18 De ira regis et suorum ad Patricium et plaga Dei super eos et transfinctione Patricii coram gentilibus.
19 De adventu Patricii in die pascae ad Temoriam et fide Dubthaich maccu Lugir.
20 De conflictu Patricii adversus magum in illa die et mirabilibus virtutibus.
21 De conversione Loiguiri regis et de verbo Patricii de regno eius post se.
22 De doctrina et babtismate signisque sancti Patricii secundum exemplum Christi.

23 De Macc Cuill et conversione eius ad verbum Patricii.
24 De gentibus laborantibus die dominica trans praeceptum Patricii.
25 De fabula Dairi et equo et oblatione Airddmache ad Patricium.
26 De fructifera terra in salsuginem versa.
27 De morte Moneisen Saxonissae.
28 De eo quod sanctus Patricius vidit caelum apertum et Filium Dei et anguelos Eius.
29 De conflictu sancti Patricii adversum Coirthech regem Aloo.

Haec pauca de sancti Patricii peritia et virtutibus Muirchu maccu Machtheni, dictante Aiduo Slebtiensis civitatis episcopo, conscripsit.

1 Patricius, qui et Sochet vocabatur, Brito natione, in Britannis natus, Cualfarnio diacono ortus, filio, ut ipse ait, Potiti presbyteri, qui fuit vico Bannavem Taburniae, haud procul a mari nostro, quem vicum constanter indubitanterque comperimus esse † ventre †*, matre etiam conceptus Concessa nomine.
Annorum xvi. puer cum ceteris captus, in hanc barbarorum insulam advectus est et apud quendam gentilem immitemque regem in servitute detentus. Qui sexennium more Hebraico ⟨in ea captivitate exegit⟩*, cum timore Dei et tremore, secundum psalmiste sententiam, in vigiliis et orationibus multis. Cencies in die et cencies in nocte orabat, libenter reddens ⟨quae Dei sunt Deo et quae Caesaris Caesari⟩*, incipiensque timere Deum et amare omnipotentem

Dominum; nam usque ad id temporis ignorabat Deum verum, sed tunc spiritus fervebat in eo.

Post multas ibi tribulationes, post famem et sitim, post frigora et nuditates, post pascenda pecora, post frequentias angeli Victorici a Deo ad illum missi, post magnas virtutes omnibus pene notas, post responsa divina (e quibus unum aut duo haec exempli tantum gracia demonstrabo: 'Bene ieiunas, cito iturus ad patriam tuam;' et iterum: 'Ecce navis tua parata est;' quae non erat prope, sed forte habebat ducenta milia passuum, ubi numquam habuerat iter) — post haec omnia, ut diximus, quae enumerari poene a nemine possunt, cum ignotis barbaris gentilibusque hominibus multos et falsos deos adorantibus iam in nave sibi parata, deserto terreno gentilique rege* cum actibus suis et accepto caelesti eternoque Deo, in comitatu sancti Spiritus ex praecepto divino* aetatis suae anno xxiii. ad Britanias navigavit.

2   Ternis itaque diebus totidemque noctibus quasi ad modum Ionae in mari cum iniquis fluctuans, postea bis denis simul et octenis diurnis luminibus Moysico more, alio licet sensu, per desertum fatigatus, murmurantibus gentilibus quasi Iudei fame et siti pene deficientibus, compulsus a gubernatore, temptatus atque ut illis Deum suum ne perirent oraret rogatus, mortalibus exoratus, turmae misertus, spiritu contribulatus, merito coronatus, a Deo magnificatus, abundantiam cibi ex grege porcorum a Deo misso sibi velut ex coturnicum turma Deo adiuvante prebuit. Mel quoque silvestre ut quondam Iohanni subvenit, motatis tamen pessimorum gentilium merito porcinis carnibus pro locustarum usu. Ille autem sanctus Patricius nichil gustans de his cibis, immolaticum enim erat, nec esuriens nec sitiens mansit illesus. Eadem vero nocte dormiens, temptavit eum satanas graviter, fingens saxa ingentia et quasi comminuens iam membra eius; sed invocato Helia bina voce, ortus est ei sol qui refulgens expulit omnes caliginum tenebras et restitutae sunt ei vires eius.

3   Et iterum post multos annos capturam ab alienigenis pertulit. Ubi prima nocte audire meruit responsum divinum sibi dicens: 'Duobus mensibus eris cum illis, id est cum inimicis tuis.' Quod ita factum est. Sexagesimo enim die liberavit eum Dominus de manibus eorum, previdens ei cum comitibus suis cibum et ignem et siccitatem quottidie, donec decimo die pervenerunt ad homines.

4   Et iterum post paucos annos ut antea in patria sua propria apud parentes suos requievit, qui ut filium receperunt, rogantes illum ut vel sic post tantas tribulationes et temptationes de reliquo vitae numquam ab illis discederet. Sed ille non consensit. Et ibi ostensae

sunt ei multae visiones.

5 Et erat annorum triginta, secundum apostolum 'in virum perfectum ⟨occurrens, in mensuram aetatis⟩* plenitudinis Christi.' Egressus ad sedem apostolicam visitandam et honorandam, ad caput utique* omnium ecclesiarum totius mundi, ut sapientiam divinam* sanctaque misteria ad quae vocavit illum Deus disceret atque intellegeret et impleret, et ut predicaret et donaret divinam gratiam in nationibus externis convertens ad fidem Christi.

6 Transnavigato igitur mari dextro Britannico ac coepto itinere per Gallias*, Alpes ad extremum, ut corde proposuerat, transcensurus, quendam sanctisimum episcopum Alsiodori civitate principem Germanum, ⟨Galliarum paene omnium⟩ summum dominum*, invenit. Aput quem non parvo tempore demoratus, iuxta id quod Paulus ad pedes Gamaliel fuerat, in omni subiectione et patientia atque oboedientia scientiam, sapientiam castitatemque et omnem utilitatem tam spiritus quam animae cum magno Dei timore et amore, in bonitate et simplicitate cordis, corpore et spiritu virgo,* toto animi desiderio didicit, dilexit, custodivit.

7 Peractisque* ibi multis temporibus quasi, ut alii, quadraginta, alii, triginta annis, ille antiquitus amicus valde fidelis*, Victoricus nomine, qui omnia sibi in Hibernica servitute possito antequam essent dixerat, eum crebris vissionibus vissitavit, dicens ei adesse tempus ut veniret et aevanguelico rete nationes feras et barbaras, ad quas docendas misserat illum Deus, ut piscaret; ibique ei dictum· est in vissione: 'Vocant te filii et filiae silvae Foclitae;' et caetera.

8 Oportuno ergo tempore imperante, comitante divino auxilio, coeptum ingreditur iter ad opus in quod ollim preparatus fuerat, utique aevanguelii. Et missit Germanus seniorem cum ullo, hoc est Segitium prespiterum, ut testem et comitem haberet, quia nec adhuc a sancto domino Germano in pontificali gradu ordinatus est. Certi etenim erant* quod Palladius, archidiaconus pape Caelestini urbis Romae episcopi, qui tunc tenebat sedem apostolicam quadragensimus quintus a sancto Petro apostolo, ille Palladius ordinatus et missus fuerat ad hanc insolam sub brumali rigore possitam convertendam. Sed prohibuit illum Deus*, quia nemo potest accipere quicquam de terra nisi datum ei fuerit de caelo. Nam neque hii feri et inmites homines facile receperunt doctrinam eius, neque et ipse voluit transegere tempus in terra non sua; sed reversus est ad eum qui missit illum. Revertente vero eo hinc et primo mari transito coeptoque terrarum itenere, in Britonum* finibus vita functus est.*

9 Audita itaque morte sancti Paladii in Britannis, quia discipuli Paladii, id est Augustinus et Benedictus et caeteri, redeuntes retulerant in Ebmoria de morte eius, Patricius et qui cum eo erant declinaverunt iter ad quendam mirabilem hominem summum episcopum, Amathoregem nomine, in propinquo loco habitantem. Ibique sanctus Patricius, sciens quae eventura erant illi,* episcopalem gradum ab Amathorege sancto episcopo accepit; sed etiam Auxilius Iserninusque et caeteri inferioris gradus eodem die quo sanctus Patricius ordinatus est. Tum acceptis benedictionibus, perfectisque omnibus secundum morem, cantato etiam Patricio quasi specialiter et convenienter hoc psalmistae vorsu: 'Tu es sacerdos in aeternum secundum ordinem Melchesedec;' venerabilis viator paratam navim in nomine sanctae Trinitatis ascendit et pervenit Brittannias; et omissis omnibus ambulandi anfractibus praeter commone viae officium (nemo enim dissidia quaerit Dominum), cum omni velocitate flatuque prospero mare nostrum contendit.

10 In illis autem diebus quibus haec gesta sunt in praedictis regionibus fuit rex quidam magnus, ferox gentilisque imperator barbarorum regnans in Temoria, quae erat caput Scotorum, Loiguire nomine, filius Neill, origo stirpis regiae totius paene * insolae. Hic autem scivos et magos et aurispices et incantatores et omnis malae artis inventores habuerat, qui poterant omnia scire et providere ex more gentilitatis et idolatriae antequam essent; e quibus hii duo prae caeteris praeferebantur, quorum nomina haec sunt, Lothroch qui et Lochru, et Lucetmael qui et Ronal.

Et hii duo ex sua arte magica crebrius profetabant morem quendam exterum futurum in modum regni cum ignota quadam doctrina molesta de* longuinquo trans maria advectum, a paucis dictatum, a multis susceptum, ab omnibusque honoratum, regna subversurum, resistentes reges occisurum*, turbas seducturum, omnes eorum deos distructurum, et eiectis omnibus illorum artis opibus in saecula regnaturum. Portantem quoque suadentemque hunc morem signaverunt et profetaverunt hiis verbis quasi in modum versiculi crebro ab hiisdem dictis, maxime in antecedentibus adventum Patricii duobus aut tribus annis. Haec autem sunt versiculi verba, propter linguae idioma* non tam manifesta:
'Adveniet Asciciput cum suo ligno† curvicipite et sua domu capite perforata.†* Incantabit nefas a sua mensa ex anteriore parte domus suae; respondebit ei sua familia tota:"Fiat, fiat." ' (Quod nostris verbis potest manifestius exprimi). 'Quando ergo haec omnia fient, regnum nostrum, quod est gentile, non stabit.'

Quod sic postea evenerat. Eversis enim in adventu Patricii idulorum culturis, fides Christi catholica nostra replevit omnia. De his ista sufficiant; redeamus ad propossitum.

11 Consummato igitur navigio sancto perfectoque, honerata navis sancti cum transmarinis mirabilibus spiritalibusque tessauris, quasi in oportunum portum, in regiónes Coolennorum in portum apud nos clarum, qui vocatur Hostium Dee, dilata est. Ubi vissum est ei nihil perfectius esse quam ut semetipsum primitus redemeret, et inde appetens sinistrales fines ad illum hominem gentilem Milcoin apud quem quondam in captivitate fuerat, portansque ei geminum servitutis pretium, terrenum utique et caeleste, ut de captivitate liberaret illum cui ante captivus servierat, ad anteriorem insolam; quae eius nomine usque hodie nominatur, prurim navis convertit. Tum de inde Brega Conalneosque fines, necnon et fines Ulathorum in levo dimitiens, ad extremum in* fretum quod est Brene se inmisit. Et descenderunt in terram ad hostium Slain ille et qui cum eo erant in navi, et absconderunt naviculam, et venierunt aliquantulum in regionem ut requiescerent ibi.

Et invenit eos porcinarius cuiusdam vjri natura boni, licet gentilis, cui nomen erat Dichu, habitans ibi ubi nunc est Orreum Patricii nomine cognominatum. Porcinarius autem putans eos fures ac latrones, exivit et indicavit domino suo Dudichoin et induxit illum super eos ignorantibus illis. Qui corde propossuerat occidere eos, sed videns faciem sancti Patricii, convertit Dominus ad bonum cogitationes eius. Et praedicavit Patricius fidem illi, et ibi credidit Patricio, et requievit ibi sanctus apud illum non multis diebus.

Sed volens cito ire ut vissitaret praedictum hominem Milcoin et portaret ei pretium suum et vel sic converteret ad Christi fidem, relicta ibi navis apud Dichoin, coepit per terras diregere viam in regiones Cruidnenorum donec pervenit ad montem Miss. De quo monte multo ante, tempore quo ibi captivus servierat, presso vestigio in petra alterius montis, expedito gradu vidit angelum Victoricum in conspectu eius ascendisse in caelum.

12 Audiens autem Miliucc servum suum iterum venire* ad vissitandum eum, ut morem quem nolebat in fine vitae faceret quasi per vim, ne servo subiectus fieret et ille sibi dominaret, instinctu diabuli sponte se igni tradidit et in domu in qua prius habitaverat rex, congregato ad se omni instrumento substantiae suae, incensus est.

Stans autem sanctus Patricius in praedicto loco a latere dextero montis

Miss, ubi primum illam regionem in qua servivit cum tali gratia adveniens vidit (ubi nunc usque crux habetur in signum), ad vissum primum illius regionis ilico sub oculis rogum regis incensum intuitus. Stupefactus igitur ad hoc opus duabus aut tribus fere horis nullum verbum proferens, suspirans et gemens lacrimansque atque haec verba promens ait: 'Nescio, Deus scit, hic homo rex qui se ipsum igni tradidit ne crederet in fine vitae suae et ne serviret Deo aeterno, nescio, Deus scit, nemo de filiis eius sedebit rex super sedem regni eius a generatione in generationem; insuper et semen eius serviet in sempiternum.'

Et his dictis, orans et armans se signo crucis, convertit cito iter suum ad regionem Ulothorum per eadem vestigia quibus venerat, et rursum pervenit in campum Inis ad Dichoin; ibique mansit diebus multis et circumiit totum campum et elegit et amavit, et coepit fides crescere ibi.

13 Adpropinquavit autem pascha in diebus illis, quod pasca primum Deo in nostra Aegipto huius insolae velut quondam in Gessen* celebratum est. Et inierunt* consilium ubi hoc primum pasca in gentibus ad quas missit illos Deus celebrarent, multisque super hac re consiliis iectis, postremo inspirato divinitus sancto Patricio vissum est hanc magnam Domini sollempnitatem quasi caput omnium sollempnitatum in campo maximo, ubi erat regnum maximum nationum harum †quod erat omnis gentilitatis et idolatriae caput, celebrari,†* ut hic invictus cuneus in caput totius idolatriae, ne possit ulterius adversus Christi fidem insurgere, sub malleo fortis operis cum fide iuncti sancti Patricii et suorum manibus primus inlideretur; et sic factum est.

14 Elevata igitur navis ad mare, et dimisso in fide plena et pace bono illo viro Dichu, migrantes de campo Iniss dexteraque manu demittentes omnia ad plenitudinem ministerii quae erant ante non incongrue leva, in portum Hostii Colpdi bene et prospere delati sunt. Relictaque ibi navi, pedistri itenere venierunt in praedictum maximum campum, donec postremo ad vesperum pervenierunt ad Ferti virorum Feec, quam, ut fabulae ferunt, foderunt viri, id est servi, Feecol Ferchertni, qui fuerat unus e novim magis prophetis Bregg. Fixoque ibi tentorio, debeta pascae vota sacrificiumque laudis cum omni devotione sanctus Patricius cum suis Deo altissimo secundum profetae vocem reddidit.

15 Contigit vero in illo anno idolatriae sollempnitatem, quam gentiles incantationibus multis et magicis inventionibus nonnullisque aliis idolatriae superstitionibus, congregatis etiam regibus, satrapis, ducibus,

principibus et optimatibus populi, insuper et magis, incantatoribus, auruspicibus et omnis artis omnisque doli* inventoribus doctoribusve vocatis ad Loigaireum velut quondam ad Nabcodonossor regem, in Temoria, istorum Babylone, exercere consuerant, eadem nocte qua sanctus Patricius pasca, illi illam adorarent exercerentque festivitatem gentilem. Erat quoque quidam mos apud illos, per edictum omnibus intimatus, ut quicumque in cunctis regionibus sive procul sive iuxta in illa nocte incendisset ignem antequam in domu regia, id est in palatio Temoriae, succenderetur, periret anima eius de populo suo.

Sanctus ergo Patricius, sanctum pasca celebrans, incendit divinum ignem valde lucidum et benedictum, qui in nocte reffulgens a cunctis pene per planitiem campi habitantibus vissus est. Accidit ergo ut a Temoria videretur, vissoque eo conspexerunt omnes et mirati sunt. Convocatisque senioribus et maioribus natu et magis, dixit eis rex: 'Quid est hoc? Quis est qui hoc nefas ausus est facere in regno meo? Pereat ille morte.' Et respondentibus omnibus senioribus et maioribus natu* regi nesciisse illum qui hoc fecerit, magi responderunt: 'Rex, in aeternum vive. Hic ignis quem videmus quique in hac nocte accensus est antequam succenderetur in domu tua, id est in palatio Temoriae, nissi extinctus fuerit in nocte hac qua accensus est, nunquam extinguetur in aeternum; insuper et omnes ignes nostrae consuitudinis supergradietur; et ille qui incendit et regnum superveniens a quo incensus est in hac nocte superabit nos omnes et te, et omnes homines regni tui seducet et cadent ei omnia regna, et ipsum implebit omnia et regnabit in saecula saeculorum.'

16 His ergo auditis turbatus est rex Loiguire valde, ut olim Erodis, et omnis civitas Temoria cum eo. Et respondens dixit: 'Non sic erit; sed nunc nos ibimus ut videamus exitum rei, et retinebimus et occidemus facientes tantum nefas in nostrum regnum.' Iunctis igitur ter novem* curribus secundum deorum traditionem et assumptis his duobus magis ad conflictionem prae omnibus optimis, id est Lucetmael et Lochru, in fine noctis illius perrexit Loiguire de Temoria ad Ferti virorum Feec, hominum et equorum facies secundum congruum illis sensum ad levam vertentes.

Euntibus autem illis, dixerunt magi regi: 'Rex, nec tu ibis ad locum in quo ignis est incensus, ne forte tu postea adoraveris illum qui incendit; sed eris foris iuxta, et vocabitur ad te ille ut te adoraverit et tu ipse dominatus fueris, et sermocinabimur ad invicem nos et ille in conspectu tuo, rex, et probabis nos sic.' Et respondens rex ait: 'Bonum consilium invenistis; sic faciam ut locuti fuistis.' Et pervenerunt ad

praefinitum locum, discendentibusque illis de curribus suis et equis,
non intraverunt in circuitum loci incensi, sed sederunt iuxta.

17 Et vocatus est sanctus Patricius ad regem extra locum incensi.
Dixeruntque magi ad suos: 'Nec surgemus nos in adventu istius; nam
quicunque surrexerit ad adventum istius credet ei postea et adorabit
eum.' Surgens denique sanctus Patricius et videns multos currus et
equos eorum, huncque psalmistae versiculum non incongrue in labiis
et in corde decantans: 'Hii in curribus et hii in equis, nos autem in
nomine Dei nostri ambulabimus;' venit ad illos. Illi non surrexerunt
in adventu eius; sed unus tantum a Domino adiutus, qui noluit
oboedire dictis magorum, hoc est Ercc filius Dego, cuius nunc
reliquiae adorantur in illa civitate quae vocatur Slane, surrexit; et
benedixit eum Patricius, et credidit Deo aeterno.

Incipientibusque illis sermocinari ad invicem, alter magus, nomine
Lochru, procax erat in conspectu sancti, audens detrachere fidei
catholicae tumulentis verbis. Hunc autem intuens turvo oculo talia
promentem sanctus Patricius, ut quondam Petrus de Simone, cum
quadam potentia et magno clamore confidenter ad Dominum dixit:
'Domine, qui omnia potes et in tua potestate consistunt, quique me
missisti huc, hic impius qui blasfemat nomen tuum elevetur nunc
foras et cito moriatur.' Et his dictis, elivatus est in aethera magus et
iterum dimissus foras desuper, verso ad lapidem cerebro, comminutus
et mortuus fuerat coram eis; et timuerunt gentiles.

18 Iratusque cum suis rex Patricio super hoc, voluit eum occidere et
dixit: 'Iniecite manus in istum perdentem nos.' Tunc videns gentiles
impios inruituros in eum, sanctus Patricius surrexit claraque voce
dixit: 'Exsurgat Deus et dissipentur inimici eius, et fugiant qui oderunt
eum a facie eius.' Et statim inruerunt tenebrae et commotio quaedam
horribilis, et expugnaverunt impii semetipsos alter adversus alterum
insurgens; et terrae motus magnus factus est, et collocavit axes
curruum eorum et agebat eos cum vi, et praecipitaverunt se currus et
equi per planitiem campi, donec ad extremum pauci ex eis semivivi
evasserunt ad montem Monduirn. Et prostrati sunt ab hac plaga
coram rege et suis senioribus* ad maledictum Patricii septem septies
viri, donec ipse remanserat †cum septem tantum hominibus, ipse et
uxor eius et duos reges et alii ex sociis quattuor†*. Et timuerunt valde.

Veniensque regina ad Patricium dixit ei: 'Homo iuste et potens, ne
perdas regem; veniens enim rex genua flectet et adorabit Dominum
tuum.' Et venit rex timore coactus et flexit genua coram sancto et

finxit se adorare quem nolebat. Et postquam separaverunt ad invicem, paululum gradiens vocavit rex sanctum Patricium simulato verbo, volens interficere eum quo modo. Sciens autem Patricius cogitationes regis pessimi, benedictis in nomine Iesu Christi sociis suis octo viris cum puero, venit ad regem. Enumerat eos rex venientes, statimque nusquam comparuerunt ab oculis regis dempti;* sed viderunt gentiles octo tantum cervos cum hynulo euntes quasi ad dissertum. Et rex Loiguire mestus, timidus et ignominiossus cum paucis evadentibus ad Temoriam reversus est deluculo.

19 Sequenti vero die, hoc est in die pascae, recumbentibus regibus et principibus et magis apud Loiguire (festus enim dies maximus apud eos erat), manducantibus illis et bibentibus vinum in palatio Temoriae sermocinantibusque aliis et aliis cogitantibus de his quae facta fuerant, sanctus Patricius cum quinque tantum viris,* ut contenderet et verbum faceret de fide sancta in Temoria coram omnibus nationibus, hostiis clausis, secundum id quod de Christo legitur, venit.

Adveniente ergo eo in caenacolum Temoriae nemo de omnibus ad adventum eius surrexit praeter unum tantum, id est Dubthoch Maccu Lugil, poetam optimum, apud quem tunc temporis ibi erat quidam adoliscens poeta, nomine Feec, qui postea mirabilis episcopus fuit, cuius reliquiae adorantur *hi* Sleibti. Hic, ut dixi, Dubthach solus ex gentibus in honorem sancti Patricii surrexit; et benedixit ei sanctus, crediditque primus in illa die Deo, et repputatum est ei ad iustitiam. Visso itaque Patricio, vocatus est a gentibus ad vescendum, ut probarent eum in venturis rebus. Ille autem, sciens quae ventura essent, non reffellit vesci.

20 Caenantibus autem omnibus, ille magus Lucet mail, qui fuerat in nocturna conflictione, etiam in illa die solicitus est extincto consocio suo confligere adversus sanctum Patricium; et ut initium causae haberet, intuentibus aliis inmissit aliquid ex vasse suo in poculum Patricii, ut probaret quid faceret. Vidensque sanctus Patricius hoc probationis genus, videntibus cunctis benedixit poculum suum, et versus est liquor in modum gelu; et conversso vasse cecidit gutta illa tantum quam inmisserat magus. Et iterum benedixit poculum; conversus est liquor in naturam, et mirati sunt omnes.

Et post paululum ait magus: 'Faciamus signa in hoc campo maximo.' Respondensque Patricius ait: 'Quae?' Et dixit magus: 'Inducamus nivem super terram.' Et ait Patricius:* 'Nolo contraria voluntati Dei inducere.' Et dixit magus: 'Ego inducam videntibus cunctis.' Tunc incantationes magicas exorsus induxit nivem super totum campum pertinguentem *ferenn*; et viderunt omnes et mirati sunt. Et ait sanctus: 'Ecce videmus hoc; depone nunc.' Et dixit: 'Ante istam horam cras non possum deponere.' Et ait sanctus: 'Potes malum et non bonum facere. Non sic ego.' Tunc benedicens per totum circuitum campum, dicto citius absque ulla pluia aut nebulis aut vento evanuit nix. Et clamaverunt turbae et mirati sunt et compuncti sunt corde.*

Et paulo post invocatis demonibus induxit magus densissimas tenebras super terram in signum; et mormuraverunt omnes. Et ait sanctus: 'Expelle tenebras.' At ille similiter non poterat. Sanctus autem orans benedixit, et reppente expulsae sunt tenebrae et refulsit sol. Et exclamaverunt omnes et gratias egerunt. His autem omnibus in conspectu regis inter magum Patriciumque gestis, ait rex ad illos: 'Libros vestros in aquam mittite, et illum cuius libri inlessi evasserunt adorabimus.' Respondit Patricius: 'Faciam ego.' Et dixit magus:''Nolo ego ad iudicium aquae venire cum isto; aquam enim Deum habet.' (Certe audivit babtisma per aquam a Patricio datum). Et respondens rex ait: 'Permitte per ignem.' Et ait Patricius: 'Prumptus sum.' At magus nolens dixit: 'Hic homo versa vice in alternos annos nunc aquam, nunc ignem deum veneratur.' Et ait sanctus: 'Non sic. Sed tu ipse ibis, et unus ex meis pueris ibit tecum in separatam et conclaussam domum, et meum erga te et tuum erga meum puerum* erit vestimentum, et sic simul incendemini.'

Et hoc consilium insedit, et aedificata est eis domus cuius dimedium ex materia viridi et alterum dimedium ex arida facta est. Et missus est magus in illam domum in partem eius viridem cum casula Patricii erga eum,* et unus e pueris sancti Patricii, Bineus nomine, cum veste magica in partem domus aridam.* Conclussa itaque extrinsecus domus coram omni turba incensa est. Et factum est in illa hora, orante Patricio, ut consumeret flamma ignis magum cum demedia domu viridi, permanente cassula sancti Patricii tantum intacta, quam ignis non tetigit. Felix autem Benineus e contrario cum demedia domu arida; secundum quod de tribus pueris dictum est, non tetigit eum ignis neque contristatus est nec quicquam molesti intulit; cassula tantum magi, quae erga eum fuerat, non sine Dei nutu exusta.

Et iratus est valde rex adversus Patricium de morte magi sui, et inruit poene in eum volens occidere; sed prohibuit illum Deus. Ad precem enim Patricii et ad vocem eius discendit ira Dei in populum inpium, et perierunt multi ex eis. Et ait sanctus Patricius regi: 'Nisi nunc credideris, cito morieris, quia descendet* ira Dei in verticem tuum.' Et timuit rex vehementer, et commotum est cor eius, et omnis civitas cum eo.

21 Congregatis igitur senioribus et omni senatu suo, dixit eis rex Loiguire: 'Melius est credere me quam mori.' Initoque consilio, ex suorum praecepto credidit in illa die et convertit ad Dominum Deum aeternum; et ibi crediderunt multi alii. Et ait sanctus Patricius ad regem: 'Quia resististi doctrinae meae et fuisti scandalum mihi, licet prolonguentur dies regni tui, nullus tamen erit ex semine tuo rex in aeternum post te.'

22 Sanctus autem Patricius, secundum praeceptum Domini Iesu iens et docens omnes* gentes babtitzansque eas in nomine Patris et Filii et Spiritus sancti, profectus a Temoria praedicavit Domino cooperante et sermonem confirmante sequentibus signis.

The Brussels and Vienna MSS (B and C) begin book 2 after this point.

23 Erat quidam homo in regionibus Ulothorum Patricii tempore, Macuil Maccugreccae nomine*, et erat hic homo valde impius, saevus tyrannus, ut Cyclops nominaretur. Cogitationibus pravus, verbis intemperatus, factis malignus, spiritu amarus, animo iracondus, corpore scelestus, mente crudelis, vita gentilis, conscientia immanis,* in tantum vergens impietatis in profundum ita ut die quadam in montosso, aspero altoque sedens loco Hindruim Moccuechach, ubi ille tyrannidem cotidie exercebat signa sumens nequissima crudelitatis et transeuntes hospites crudeli scelere interficiens, sanctum quoque Patricium claro fidei lumine radiantem et miro quodam caelestis gloriae deademate fulgentem, videns eum inconcussa doctrinae fiducia per cóngruum viae iter ambulantem, interficere cogitaret, dicens satilitibus suis: 'Ecce, seductor ille et perversor hominum venit, cui mos facere praestigias ut decipiat homines multosque seducat. Eamus ergo et temptemus eum, et sciemus si habet potentiam aliquam ille Deus in quo se gloriatur.'

Temptaveruntque virum sanctum in hoc modo*; posuerunt unum ex semetipsis sanum in medio eorum sub sago iacentem infirmitatemque mortis simulantem, ut probarent sanctum in huiusquemodi fallaci re, sanctum seductorem, virtutes praestigias, et orationes veneficia vel incantationes nominantes. Adveniente sancto Patricio cum discipulis suis, gentiles dixerunt ei: 'Ecce, unus ex nobis nunc infirmatus est. Accede itaque ~t canta super eum aliquas incantationes sectae tuae, si forte sanari possit.' Sanctus Patricius, sciens omnes dolos et fallacias eorum, constanter et intripide ait: 'Nec mirum si infirmus fuisset.' Et revelantes socii eius faciem insimulantis infirmitatem, viderunt eum iam mortuum. At illi obstupescentes ammirantesque tale miraculum, dixerunt intra se gementes:* 'Vere hic homo Dei est; male fecimus temptantes eum.'

Sanctus vero Patricius conversus ad Maccuil ait: 'Quare temptare me voluisti?' Respondensque ille tyrannus crudelis ait: 'Poeniteat me facti huius, et quodcumque praeciperis mihi faciam, et trado me nunc in potentiam Dei tui excelsi quem praedicas.' Et ait sanctus! 'Crede ergo in Deo meo Domino Iesu, et confitere peccata tua et babtitzare in nomine Patris et Filii et Spiritus sancti.' Et conversus in illa hora credidit Deo aeterno, babtitzatusque est. Insuper et haec* addidit Maccuil dicens: 'Confiteor tibi, sancte domine mi Patrici, quod proposui te interficere. Iudica ergo quantum debuerit pro tanto ac tali cremine.'

Et ait Patricius: 'Non possum iudicare, sed Deus iudicabit. Tu tamen egredire nunc inermis ad mare, et transi velociter de regione hac Hibernensi, nihil tollens tecum de tua substantia praeter vile et parvum indumentum quo possit corpus tuum contegi, nihil gustans nihilque bibens de fructu insolae huius, habens insigne peccati tui in capite tuo; et postquam pervenias ad mare, conliga pedes tuos conpede ferreo, et proiece clavim eius in mari, et mitte te in navim unius pellis absque gubernaculo et absque remo, et quocumque te duxerit ventus et mare esto paratus, et terram in quamcumque defferat te divina providentia, inhabita et exerce ibi divina mandata.' Dixitque Maccuill: 'Sic faciam ut dixisti. De viro autem mortuo quid faciemus?' Et ait Patricius: 'Vivet et exsurget sine dolore.' Et suscitavit eum Patricius in illa hora, et revixit sanus.

Et migravit inde Maccuil tam cito ad mare dexterum campi Inis, habeta fiducia inconcussa fidei, collegavitque se in litore ieciens clavim in mare secundum quod praeceptum est ei, et ascendit mare in navicula. Et inspiravit illi ventus aquilo et sustulit eum ad meridiem iecitque eum in insolam, Evoniam nomine. Invenitque ibi duos viros valde mirabiles, in fide et doctrina fulgentes, qui primi docuerunt verbum Dei et babtismum in Evonia, et conversi sunt homines insolae in doctrina eorum ad fidem catholicam, quorum nomina sunt

Conindri et Rumili. Hii vero videntes virum unius habitus mirati sunt et miserti sunt illius, elivaveruntque de mari suscipientes cum gaudio. Ille igitur, ubi inventi sunt spiritales patres in regione a Deo sibi credita, ad regulam eorum corpus et animam exercuit, et totum vitae tempus exegit apud istos duos sanctos episcopos, usque dum successor eorum in episcopatu effectus est. Hic est Maccuil *dimane* episcopus et antestes Arddae Huimnonn.

24 Alia vero vice sanctus requiescens Patricius in die dominica supra mare iuxta salsuginem quae est ad aquilonalem plagam a Collo Bovis distans non magno viae* spatio, audivit sonum intemperatum gentilium in die dominica laborantium, facientium *rathi,* vocatisque illis prohibuit eos Patricius ne laborarent in dominico die. At illi non consentiebant verbis sancti; quin immo inridentes deludebant eum. Et ait sanctus Patricius: 'Mudebroth, quamvis laboraveritis, nec tamen proficiat.' Quod tamen completum est. In sequenti enim nocte ventus magnus adveniens turbavit mare, et omne opus gentilium destruxit tempestas, iuxta verbum sancti.

25 Fuit quidam homo dives et honorabilis in regionibus Orientalium cui nomen erat Daire. Hunc autem rogavit Patricius ut aliquem locum ad exercendam religionem daret ei. Dixitque dives ad sanctum: 'Quem locum petis?' 'Peto,' inquit sanctus, 'ut illam altitudinem terrae quae nominatur Dorsum Salicis dones mihi, et construam ibi locum.' At ille noluit sancto terram illam dare altam, sed dedit illi locum alium in inferiori terra, ubi nunc est *Fertae* Martyrum iuxta Ardd machae, et habitavit ibi sanctus Patricius cum suis.

Post vero aliquod tempus venit eques † *doiri* † Dairi ducens equum suum mirabilem,* ut pasceretur in herbosso loco Christianorum. Et offendit Patricium talis dilatio equi in locum suum, et ait: 'Stulte fecit Daire bruta mittens animalia turbare locum parvum quem dedit Deo.' At vero eques tanquam sordus non audiebat et sicut mutus non aperiens os suum nihil loquebatur, sed dimisso ibi equo nocte illa exivit. Crastino autem die mane veniens eques vissitare equum suum, invenit eum iam mortuum. Domique reversus tristis ait ad dominum suum: 'Ecce, Christianus ille occidit equum tuum. Offendit enim illum turbatio loci sui.' Et dixit Daire: 'Occidatur et ille; nunc ite et interficite eum.'

Euntibus autem illis foras, dictu citius inruit mors super Daire. Et ait uxor eius: 'Causa Christiani est haec mors.* Eat quis cito, et portentur nobis beneficia eius, et salvus eris; et prohibeantur* et revocentur qui

exierunt occidere eum.' Exieruntque duo viri ad Christianum qui
dixerunt ei, celantes quod factum est: 'Et ecce, infirmatus est Daire;
portetur illi aliquid a te, si forte sanari possit.' Sanctus autem
Patricius, sciens quae facta sunt, dixit: 'Nimirum.' Benedixitque
aquam et dedit dicens: 'Ite, aspergite equum vestrum ex aqua ista, et
portate illam vobiscum.' Et fecerunt sic, et revixit equus; et
portaverunt secum, sanatusque est Daire asparsione aquae sanctae.

Et venit Daire post haec ut honoraret sanctum Patricium, portans
secum aeneum mirabilem transmarinum metritas ternas capientem.
Dixitque Daire ad sanctum: 'Ecce hic aeneus sit tecum.' Et ait
sanctus Patricius: 'Grazacham.' Reversusque Daire ad domum suam
dixit: 'Stultus homo est qui nihil boni dixit praeter grazacham pro
aeneo mirabili metritarum trium.' Additque Daire dicens servis suis:
'Ite, reportate nobis aeneum nostrum.' Exierunt et dixerunt Patricio:
'Portabimus aeneum.' Nihilominus et illa vice sanctus Patricius dixit:
'Gratzacham, portate;' et portaverunt. Interrogavitque Daire socios
suos dicens: 'Quid dixit Christianus quando reportastis aeneum?' At
illi responderunt: 'Grazacham dixit et ille.' Daire respondens dixit:
'Gratzacham in dato, grazacham in ablato; eius dictum tam bonum
est — cum grazacham illis portabitur illi rursum aeneus suus.' Et venit
Daire ipsemet illa vice et portavit aeneum ad Patricium, dicens ei:
'Fiat tecum aeneus tuus. Constans enim et incommotabilis homo es.
Insuper et partem illam agri quam ollim petisti do tibi nunc quantum
habeo, et inhabita ibi.' Et illa est civitas quae nunc Arddmachae
nominatur.

Et exierunt ambo, sanctus Patricius et Daire, ut considerarent mirabile
oblationis et beneplacitum munus, et ascenderunt illam altitudinem
terrae, invenieruntque cervam cum vitulo suo parvo iacente in loco in
quo nunc altare est sinistralis aeclessiae in Ardd mache. Et voluerunt
comites Patricii tenere vitulum et occidere, sed noluit sanctus neque
permissit; quin potius ipsemet sanctus tenuit vitulum portans eum in
humeris suis. Et secuta illum cerva velut mitissima mansuetissimaque*
ovis usquedum dimisserat vitulum in altero saltu sito* ad aquilonalem
plagam Airdd mache, ubi usque hodie signa quaedam virtutis eius
manentia periti dicunt.

26 Virum aliquem valde durum et tam avarum in campo Inis habitantem
in tantum stultitiae avaritiaeque incurrisse cremen periti ferunt, ut
duos boves carrum* Patricii vechentes, alio die post sanctum laborem
in pastu agili sui requiescentibus pascentibusque se bobus, violenter
inconstanter praesente sancto Patricio vanus ille homo per vim coegit.

Cui irascens sanctus Patricius cum maledictione dixit: '*Mudebrod,*
male fecisti. Nusquam proficiat tibi ager hic tuus neque semini tuo in
aeternum; iam inutilis erit.' Et factum est sic. Inundatio etenim maris
tam habunda eodem veniens die circumluit et operuit totum agrum,
et positus* est iuxta profetae verbum terra fructifera in salsuginem a
malitia inhabitantis in ea. Arenossa ergo et infructuossa haec a die
qua maledixit eam sanctus Patricius usque in hodiernum diem.

27 [Itaque, volente Domino, Patricii ut ita dicam totius Hiberniae
episcopi doctorisque egregii de virtutibus pauca pluribus ennarrare
conabor.] * Quodam igitur tempore, cum tota Britannia incredulitatis
algore rigesceret, cuiusdam regis egregia filia, cui nomen erat Monesan,
Spiritus sancti repleta auxilio, cum quidam eius expeteret amplexus
coniugalis, non adquievit* ⟨neque⟩ cum aquarum multis irrigata
esset undis ad id quod nolebat et deterius erat compelli potuit. Nam
illa cum inter verbera et aquarum irrigationes solita esset interrogare*
matrem et nutricem utrum compertum haberent* rotae factorem qua
totus illuminatur mundus, et cum responsum acciperet per quod
compertum haberet solis factorem esse eum cui caelum sedes est, cum
acta esset frequenter ut coniugali vinculo copularetur, luculentissimo
Spiritus sancti ⟨consilio⟩* illustrata ⟨dicebat⟩*: 'Nequaquam
itaque hoc faciam.' Quaerebat namque per naturam totius creaturae
factorem, in hoc patriarchae Abraham secuta exemplum.

Parentes eius inito consilio a Deo sibi tributo,* audito Patricio viro ab
aeterno Deo visitari* septimo semper die, Scoticas* partes † cum
filia ⟨petentes⟩ pulsaverunt Patricium, quem tanto labore quesit-
um repererunt.†* Qui illos novicos percunctari coepit. Tunc illi viatores
clamare ceperunt et dicere: 'Cupidissimae filiae videndi Deum causa
coacti ad te venire facti sumus.' Tunc ille repletus Spiritu sancto
elevavit vocem suam et dixit ad eam: 'Si in Deum credis?' Et ait:
'Credo.' Tunc sacro Spiritus et aquae lavacro eam lavit. Nec mora;
postea solo prostrata spiritum in manus angelorum tradidit. Ubi
moritur ibi et adunatur. Tunc Patricius prophetavit quod post annos
viginti corpus illius ad propinquam cellulam de illo loco tolleretur omni
honore; quod postea ita factum est. Cuius transmarinae reliquiae ibi
adorantur usque hodie.

28 Dominici et apostolici Patricii, cuius mentionem facimus, quoddam
miraculum mirifice gestum, quod ei in carne adhuc stanti* et Stephano
poene tantum* contigisse legitur, brevi retexam relatu. Quodam
autem* tempore, cum orationis causa ad locum solitum per nocturna
spacia procederet, consueta caeli vidit miracula, suumque carissimum

ac fidelem probare volens sanctum puerum, dixit: 'O fili mi, dic
michi, quaeso, si sentis ea quae ego sentio.' Tunc parvulus, nomine
Benignus, incunctanter dixit: 'Iam mihi cognita ea quae sentis. Nam
video caelum apertum et Filium Dei et angelos eius.' Tunc Patricius
dixit: 'Iam te meum successorem dignum esse sentio.' Nec mora,
gradu concito ad suetum locum orationis pervenere.* His ergo
orantibus* in medio fluminis alveo, parvulus dixit: 'Iam algorem
aquaticum sustinere non possum.' Nam ei aqua nimis erat frigida. Tunc
dixit ei Patricius ut de superiori ⟨loco⟩* ad inferiorem descenderet.
Nichilominus ibi diu* perstare ⟨non⟩* potuit. Nam se aquam
calidam sensisse testabatur. Tunc ille non sustinens in eo loco diu
stare terram ascendit.

29 Quoddam mirabile gestum Patricii non transibo silentio. Huic
nuntiatum est nequissimum opus cuiusdam regis Britannici nomine
Corictic, infausti crudelisque tyranni. Hic namque erat maximus
persecutor interfectorque Christianorum. Patricius autem per epistolam ad viam veritatis revocare temptavit; cuius salutaria deridebat
monita. Cum autem ista* nuntiarentur Patricio, oravit Dominum et
dixit: 'Deus, si fieri potest, expelle hunc perfidum de presenti seculo-
que futuro.' Non grande postea tempus effluxerat,* et ⟨Corictic⟩*
musicam artem audivit a quodam cantari* quod ⟨cito⟩* de solio
regali transiret. Omnesque karissimi eius viri in hanc proruperunt
vocem. Tunc ille, cum esset in medio foro, ilico vulpeculae* miser-
abiliter arepta forma, profectus in suorum presentia, ex illo die
illaque hora velut fluxus aquae transiens nusquam conparuit.

TEXTUAL NOTES

Pref; Coguitosi *Hogan*: cognito si *A*

1.   ven tre *B*: Nemthor *V2V3V4*
   sexennium . . . ⟨in ea captivitate exegit⟩ *Hogan* (*cf. V2V4P*):
       sexennem *B*
   reddens ⟨quae Dei . . . Caesari⟩ *Hogan* (*cf. P*): rediens *B*
   deserto tiranno gentilique homine *B*: deserto itaque rege terreno *N*
   in comitatu sancti spiritus ex praecepto divino *Bieler*: in comitatu
       sancto excepto divino *B*: praecepito enim divino admonitus,
       spiritu sancto comitatus *N*
5.   ⟨occurrens in mensuram aetatis⟩ *P*: et cetera usque *B*
   itaque *B*
   sapienciam divinam *N*: sapiens iam divina *B*
6.   accepto itinere per Gallicas *B*: ceptoque per Gallias itinere *N*
   ⟨Galliarum paene omnium⟩ summum dominum *Bury* (*cf. V2V4P*):
       summum donum *B*
   virgo corpore et spiritu *V3* (*cf. P*): vigore *B*
7.   peractis *NV4*: factisque *B*
   antiquitus amicus valde fidelis *N*: antiquus valde fidelis *B*
8.   certi etenim erant *CNV2*: certe enim erat *A*: ceteri enim erant *B*
   Deus *om.A*
   Britonum *AV3*: Pictorum *CBNPV2V4*
   functus est *CB*: factus *A*
9.   illi *CBP*: ibi *A*: sibi *V2*: ei *V4*
10. pene totius *Bury*: huius pene *A*
    de *om.A*
    reges occisurum *CBNV2V4*: *om.A*
    propter linguae idioma *CB*: pro linguae idiomo *A*
    curvicipite *CN*: curvi capite *A*: curvo capite *B*: et sua domu
        White: ex sua (ex ea sua *C*) domu *ACBN*: capite perforata *B*:
        capita perforata *C*: capite perforato *AN*
11. in *CB*: *om.A*
12. iterum *AB*: iterum reversum *V3*: iturum *Hogan*: venire *N*
        (*cf. PV2V4*)

13. Gessen *Gwynn.(cf. V2P)*: Genesseon *A*: Genesim *B*
    inierunt *NPV2V4*: ininierunt *B*: invenierunt *A*
    quod erat omnis gentilitatis et idolatriae ne possit ulterius liberari
        A: ubi maxime caput gentilitatis et idolatriae praestiterat
        censuit celebrari *V2V4 (cf. P)*: quod erat omnis gentilitatis et
        idolatriae caput draconis confringeret a servis Dei excelsi
        celebrari *B*
15. doli *Hogan*: doni *A*
    et magis . . . maioribus natu *om.A*
16. ergo ter novam *P*: igitur ternis novies *V2V4*: ergo . . . ternis nonies
        B: ternis nonisque *N*
18. ac suis senioribus *B*: ex suis sermonibus *A*
    remanserat tantum hominibus ipse et uxor eius et alii ex Scotis
        duo *A*: remanserat quattuor tantum ipse et uxor eius et alii ex sociis
        duo *B (cf. V2)*: ipse rex cum septem tantum hominibus remansit
        illaesus, uxore videlicet sua et duobus regibus nec non et
        quattuor viris *P*
    dempti *BNV2*: *om.A*
19. cum *om.AB*: cum quinque viris *V2*: cum duobus tantum viris *P*:
        quinque viris comitantibus *V4*
20. Patricius *CBV2V3V4*: pater *A*
    mirati sunt et compuncti sunt corde *V3*: mirata est valde plebs et
        compuncta est corde *C (cf.NV4)*: mirati sunt corde *AP*: mirate
        sunt valde *B*
    meum puerum *PV2*: me *A*
    cum casula Patricii erga eum *C (cf. P)*: *om.AB*
    aridam *CPV3*: *om.A*: in parte domus aridae *B*
    ira Dei in populum . . . quia descendet *om.A*
22. iens et docens omnes *om.A*
23. nomine *BN (cf. PV3)*: *om.A*
    immanis *BN*: inanis *A*
    hoc modo *P*: hoc homo *B*: hoc mundo temptaverunt et *A*
    gementes *BNP*: gentes *A (cf. V3)*
    haec *Gwynn* (et haec audivit Macuil *B*): non *A*
24. viae *B*: vice *A*
25. equum suum mirabilem *Gwynn* (cum equo suo mirabili *V3*):
        equum suum miraculum *A*: equum suum et ait stulte mirabile *B*
    haec mors *BP*: haec *A*: hoc *N*
    prohibeantur *Gwynn*: prohibeant *B*: prohibentur *A*
    mitissima ac mansuetissima *P*: mitissima *NV3V4*: amantissimaque *A*
    situm *A*
26. carrarum *A*
    positus *A*: posita *NP*

27. (this sentence marks the beginning of book 2 in *B*; and follows
    there immediately after ch. 22)
    adquieum *B*
    interrogare *Hogan*: interrogabat *B*
    utrum compertum haberent *N*: uti compertum haberet *B*
    illustrata consilio *N*
    ⟨dicebat⟩ *Hogan*
    iusti tributo *B*: sibi tradito *P*
    visitato *B*
    Scoticas *Hogan*: sconas *B*
    cum filia pulsavere Patricium quem tanto labore quesitum reperire
        B: cum filia petiverunt quaerentes Patricium quem tanto labore
        quesitum reperire meruerunt *Hogan*
28. quod ei in carne adhuc stanti *Hogan*: in carne adhuc quod ei *B*
    tantum *Hogan* (tantum fere esse commune *N*): totum *B*
    ante *B*: enim *N*
    pervenere *Hogan*: pervenire *B*
    his orationibus *B*: illis ergo orantibus *N*: his ergo in oratione
        constitutis *P*
    loco *P* (*cf. N*): *om.B*
    diu *P*: duo *B*
    non *P* (*cf. N*): *om.B*
29. ista *Hogan*: ita *B*
    effluxerat *Hogan*: effluxuat *B*
    ⟨Corictic⟩ *e.g.*: praefatus ille tyrannus *P*
    cantari *N*: cantare *B*: praecantari *P*
    cito *P*: *om.BN*
    vulpeculae *PNV3*: vel ficuli *B*

LIFE

Preface

Many, my lord Aed, have attempted to organise this particular
narrative in accordance with the tradition handed down to them by
their fathers and by those who have been storytellers from the
beginning, but because of the grave difficulties involved in recounting
it and of differing opinions and numerous persons' numerous con-
jectures they have never succeeded in reaching the one sure path of
historical fact; and so, if I am not mistaken, as our people's saying
here goes, just as boys are brought into the meeting-place, so I have
brought the child's rowing-boat of my poor intellect onto this deep
and dangerous ocean of hagiography, with the waves surging in
wildly swirling walls of water, among whirlpools and jagged rocks
in uncharted seas - an ocean never yet attempted or embarked on
by any barque except only that of my father Cogitosus. However, to
avoid giving the impression that I am exaggerating, I shall, with some
reluctance, set about expounding this small and piece-meal selection
from St. Patrick's numerous acts. I have little talent, dubious
authorities, and am subject to lapses of memory; I have only feeble
insight and a poor style; but I am prompted by dutiful and loving
affection and am obedient to the command of your holiness and
dignity.

29. St. Patrick's conflict with Coroticus, king of Ail.

These few items concerning St. Patrick's experience and miraculous powers were written down by Muirchu maccu Machtheni under the direction of Aed, bishop of the town of Sletty.

1   Patrick, who was also called Sochet, was of British nationality, born in Britain, the son of the deacon Calpurnius, whose father, as Patrick himself says, was the priest Potitus, who came from the town of Bannavem Taburniae, not far from our sea; we have discovered for certain and beyond any doubt that this township is Ventre; and the mother who bore him was named Concessa.

At the age of sixteen the boy, with others, was captured and brought to this island of barbarians and was kept as a slave in the household of a certain cruel pagan king. He spent six years in captivity, in accordance with the Jewish custom, in fear and trembling before God, as the psalmist says (*Psalms 54, 6*), and in many vigils and prayers. He used to pray a hundred times a day and a hundred times a night, gladly giving to God what is due to God and to Caesar what is due to Caesar and beginning to fear God and to love the Lord Almighty; for up to that time he had no knowledge of the true God, but at this point the Spirit became fervent within him.

After many hardships there, after enduring hunger and thirst, cold and nakedness, after pasturing flocks, after visits from Victoricus, an angel sent to him by God, after great miracles known to almost everyone, after divine prophecies (of which I shall give just one or two examples: 'You do well to fast, since you will soon be going to your home country,' and again: 'See, your ship is ready,' though it was not near at hand but was perhaps two hundred miles away, where he had never been to) -after all these experiences, as we have said, which can hardly be counted by anyone, in the twenty-third year of his life he left the earthly, pagan king and his works, received the heavenly, eternal God and now sailed for Britain by God's command and accompanied by the Holy Spirit in the ship which lay ready for him; with him were barbarian strangers and pagans who worshipped many false gods.

2   So for three days and as many nights he was tossed at sea with the ungodly, like Jonah, and after that for the space of twenty-eight days he toiled through the wilderness, just as Moses did, though with a different significance; as the pagans almost collapsed from hunger and thirst, they grumbled, like the Jews. He was urged by the captain and put under pressure and asked to pray to his God for them that they should not perish; he was prevailed upon by mortal men; he took pity on the band, he was troubled in spirit, was deservedly crowned,

was magnified by God - he supplied them with an abundance of food from the herd of pigs sent him by God, just as Moses fed the Children of Israel from the flock of quails with God's help. There was also wild honey to succour them, as it once did John; however, instead of locusts pork had been substituted on account of those wicked pagans. But Patrick did not so much as taste this food, for it was a sacrificial offering, and he remained unharmed and neither hungry nor thirsty. And as he slept that night, Satan attacked him violently, forming huge rocks and as it were already crushing his limbs; but he called on the name of Helias twice, the sun rose on him and with its beams it drove away all the gloom of darkness, and his strength was restored to him.

3   Many years later he again endured captivity at the hands of foreigners. And on the first night of his capture he was privileged to hear a divine voice prophesying to him: 'For two months you will be with them, that is to say, with your enemies.' And so it came about; on the sixtieth day the Lord delivered him from their hands, providing him and his companions with food and fire and dry weather every day until on the tenth day they reached human habitation.

4   And again a few years later he settled quietly as before in his home country with his kinsfolk, who welcomed him as a son, begging him never ever, after such trials and tribulations, to leave them for the rest of his life. But he refused to agree; and he was shown many visions there.

5   And he was thirty years old, as the apostle says, 'reaching perfect manhood, the measure of the age of the fulness of Christ.' (*Ephesians 4.13*). He set out to visit and pay his respects to the apostolic see, that is, to the head of all the churches in the whole world, in order to learn and understand the divine wisdom and holy mysteries to which God called him and to fulfil them; and so that he might preach and confer divine grace on foreign peoples by converting them to faith in Christ.

6   So he crossed the southern British sea, and beginning his journey through Gaul with the intention of eventually crossing the Alps, as he had resolved in his heart, he came on a very holy bishop, Germanus, who ruled in the city of Auxerre, the greatest lord in almost all of Gaul. He stayed with him for quite some time, just as Paul sat at the feet of Gamaliel; and in all humility, patience and obedience he learned, loved and treasured wholeheartedly knowledge, wisdom, purity and every benefit to soul and spirit, with great fear and love for God, in goodness and singleness of heart and chaste in body and spirit.

7   And when he had spent a considerable time there (some say forty years, others thirty), that most faithful friend from time long past called Victoricus, who had foretold everything to him before it happened when he was in slavery in Ireland, visited him in a large number of visions, telling him that the time was at hand for him to come and fish with the net of the Gospel for the wild, barbarian peoples whom God had sent him to teach; and there he was told in a vision: 'The sons and daughters of the forest of Foclut are calling you, etc.'

8   And so, when a suitable opportunity so directed, with God's help to accompany him he set out on the journey which he had already begun, to the work for which he had long been prepared - the work, that is, of the Gospel. And Germanus sent an older man with him, namely the priest Segitius, so that Patrick would have a witness and companion, since he had not yet been consecrated to the rank of bishop by the holy lord Germanus. For they were well aware that Palladius, the archdeacon of Pope Celestine, the bishop of the city of Rome who then held the apostolic see as forty-fifth in line from St. Peter the apostle, that this Palladius had been consecrated and sent to convert this island, lying as it does in frozen wintriness. But God prevented him, because no one can receive anything from this earth unless it has been given him from heaven. For these wild, un-civilised people did not take kindly to his teaching, nor did he himself want to spend time in a land which was not his own; he returned to him who sent him. But on his return journey from here, after making the first sea crossing and proceeding by land, he died in the land of the British.

9   And so, when the word came of the death of St. Palladius in Britain, since Palladius' disciples, Augustine, Benedict and the others, returned to Ebmoria with the news of his death, Patrick and his companions turned aside to a wonderful man, a very important bishop called Amator, who lived nearby. And there St. Patrick, knowing what was to happen to him, received the rank of bishop from the holy bishop Amator, as also Auxilius and Iserninus and others received lesser orders on the same day as St. Patrick was consecrated. They received the blessings, everything was performed in the customary way, and the following verse of the psalmist was also sung, especially appropriate for Patrick: 'You are a priest for ever, in the manner of Melchisedek.' (*Psalms 109.4*). Then in the name of the holy Trinity the venerable traveller went on board the ship which had been prepared and reached Britain; and as he made his way on foot he avoided all detours, except for the ordinary business of travelling (for no one seeks the Lord by idleness), and then he hurried across our sea with all speed and

a favourable wind.

10   Now in the days in which these events took place in the aforesaid area there was a certain king, the fierce heathen emperor of the barbarians, who reigned in Tara, which was the Irish capital. His name was Loegaire, the son of Niall and the ancestor of the royal house of almost the whole of this island. He had had wise men, wizards, soothsayers, enchanters and inventors of every black art who were able in their heathen, idolatrous way to know and foresee everything before it happened; two of them were favoured above the rest, their names being Lothroch, also called Lochru, and Lucetmael, also known as Ronal.

These two repeatedly foretold by their magical arts that there would come to be a certain foreign practice like a kingdom, with some strange and troublesome doctrine; a practice brought from afar across the seas, proclaimed by a few, adopted by many and respected by all; it would overthrow kingdoms, kill kings who resisted, win over great crowds, destroy all their gods, and after driving out all the resources of their art it would reign for ever and ever. They also identified and foretold the man who would bring and urge this practice in the following words, often repeated by them in a sort of verse form, especially in the two or three years preceding Patrick's arrival. This is how the verse ran; the sense is less than clear because of the different character of the language:

'Adze-head shall come, with his crook-headed staff and his house with a hole in its head. He shall chant blasphemy from his table, from the eastern part of his house, and all his household will answer him: 'So be it, so be it!'' (This can be expressed more clearly in our own language.) 'So when all these things happen, our kingdom, which is heathen, shall not stand.'

And this is just as it later turned out. For the worship of idols was wiped out on Patrick's arrival, and the catholic faith in Christ filled every corner of our land. So much for this topic; let us return to our subject.

11   So when the holy voyage had been successfully completed, the saint's ship, laden with wonderful religious treasures from across the sea, was brought, as to a suitable harbour, to the country of the Cualann, to a harbour in fact of some repute amongst us called Inverdee. And there it seemed to him that he could do no better than first to redeem himself; and so from there he set out for the north to that pagan Miliucc in whose household he had once been in captivity, bringing him a double ransom from slavery, an earthly and an heavenly one, so as to deliver from captivity the man to whom

he had previously been enslaved as a captive. He headed the ship's bow towards the eastern island which is named after him to this day, and from there he sailed on, leaving Brega and the Conaille country and also the country of the Ulaid to his left, and finally put into the sound called Brene (Strangford Lough). And he and those on board with him landed at the mouth of the Slane, hid the ship and went a little inland to rest there.

They were discovered by the swineherd of a man called Dichu, a pagan but good at heart, who lived at the place where there is now the barn named after Patrick (Saul). And the swineherd, thinking that they were thieves and robbers, went off and informed his master Dichu and brought him on them unknown to them. He had made up his mind to kill them, but at the sight of St. Patrick's face the Lord turned his thoughts to good. And Patrick preached the faith to him and he believed Patrick there; and the saint rested there with him for a few days.

But wishing to press on and visit the aforementioned Miliucc and bring him his ransom and in that way convert him to faith in Christ, he left the ship there with Dichu and proceeded to make his way on land to the country of the Cruithne until he reached Mount Slemish. It was from this mountain that long before, when he had been in slavery as a captive there, he saw the angel Victoricus before his very eyes ascend swift-footed into heaven and leave the imprint of his step on the rock of the other mountain.

12   Now when Miliucc heard that his slave was coming back to visit him and impose on him under duress, as it were, at the end of his life a practice which he did not wish to accept, to avoid being subjected to his slave and having his slave lord it over him, at the devil's prompting he deliberately consigned himself to the flames and, gathering around him all his goods and chattels, was burned to death in the house in which he had previously lived as king.

Now as St. Patrick stood on the aforesaid spot on the south side of Mount Slemish where, coming with such divine favour, he first saw the district in which he had been a slave (to this day the place is marked by a cross), there and then at the first glimpse of the district he noticed before his eyes the king's burnt-out pyre. Dumbfounded at this deed he uttered not a word for two or almost three hours; then as he sighed and groaned and wept he spoke these words: 'I do not know, but God knows; this man, this king who consigned himself to the flames to avoid believing at the end of his life and serving the eternal God, I do not know, but God knows, none of his sons shall sit as king on the throne of his kingdom from one generation to the next; moreover his descendants shall be slaves for ever.'

So saying, he prayed, armed himself with the sign of the cross and speedily retraced his steps back to the country of the Ulaid, and he came back to Magh Inis to Dichu: he stayed there for many days and went round the whole plain and chose and loved it, and the faith began to grow there.

13   Now during those days Easter approached, the first Passover which was celebrated to God's glory in this island Egypt of ours as it once was in Goshen. And they began to discuss where they should celebrate this first Easter among the heathen to whom God had sent them. Finally, when many proposals had been made on the subject, St. Patrick had the divinely inspired idea of celebrating this great festival of the Lord, as the chief of all festivals, in the great plain where there was the greatest kingdom of these peoples, the capital of all paganism and idolatry, so that here an invincible wedge could be driven into the head of all idolatry to prevent it ever again rising against the faith of Christ, with the hammer-blows of a resolute deed linked with faith, a hammer first wielded spiritually by St. Patrick and his followers; and so it turned out.

14   So the ship was carried down to the sea, and after taking leave of the good fellow Dichu in full faith and peace, they moved on from Magh Inis and leaving on their right hand for the future fulfilment of their ministry all that had previously, not inappropriately, been to their left, they came safe and sound to the harbour of the mouth of the Boyne (Drogheda). Leaving the ship there they went on foot to the aforesaid great plain, till finally towards evening they reached the Burial Ground of the men of Fiacc (Slane), which, as legend has it, was dug by the men, that is to say, the servants of Feccol Ferchertni, who was one of the nine magician prophets of Brega. And pitching his tent there, St. Patrick rendered with his followers the due paschal vows and sacrifice of praise to the most high God with all piety, in accordance with the prophet's word.

15   It happened that this was the year in which the heathen were accustomed to hold a festival of idolatry, with many enchantments, feats of magic and various other idolatrous superstitions, before a great gathering of the kings, governors, commanders, important personages and nobility of the people, not to mention the wizards, enchanters, soothsayers and devisers and teachers of every art and deceit, who were summoned to Loegaire, as once upon a time to king Nebuchadnezzar, at Tara, their Babylon; and they happened to be observing and celebrating that pagan festival on the same night as St. Patrick was celebrating Easter. They also had a custom, which was made known to all by proclamation, that if anyone in any part of the country, be it near or

far, lit a fire before one was kindled in the king's house, in the palace of Tara, his soul would perish from among his people.

So St. Patrick, as he celebrated holy Easter, lit a divine fire, very bright and blessed, and as it gleamed in the darkness it was seen by almost all the inhabitants of the flat plain. So it came about that it was seen from Tara, and everyone gazed in amazement at the sight. The king called together the elders, councillors and wizards and said to them: 'What is this? Who is it who has dared to commit this sacrilege in my kingdom? Let him be put to death.' And when all the elders and councillors replied to the king that they did not know who had done it, the wizards replied: 'O king, live for ever. This fire which we see and which was lit this night before one was lit in your house, that is, in the palace of Tara, will never be put out ever unless it is put out this night on which it has been lit; and what is more, it will surpass all the fires of our practice; and he who lit the fire and the coming kingdom by which it was lit this night will overcome us all, and you, and will win over all the men of your kingdom, and all kingdoms will yield to it, and it will fill all things and reign for ever and ever.'

16   King Loegaire was deeply disturbed at these words, as was Herod of old, and all the city of Tara with him. In reply he said: 'It will not be so; no, we shall now go to see the end of the matter; we shall arrest and put to death those who are committing such sacrilege against our kingdom.' So yoking twenty-seven chariots as the tradition of the gods demanded and taking these two wizards, Lucetmael and Lochru, the best of all for this confrontation, Loegaire proceeded at the close of that night from Tara to the Burial Ground of the men of Fiacc (Slane), with his men and horses facing towards the left, that being the fitting direction for them.

As they went, the wizards said to the king: 'O king, you shall not go to the place where the fire has been lit, in case you afterwards do obeisance to him that lit it; no, you will be outside, near at hand, and he will be summoned to you, so that he will do obeisance to you and it will be you who will be lord and master; and we and he shall talk together in your sight, O king, and you will test us in this way.' And the king replied: 'It is a good plan you have devised; I shall do as you have said.' They reached the appointed place and dismounting from their chariots and horses they did not enter the area immediately surrounding the place where the fire had been lit, but sat down nearby.

17   St. Patrick was summoned to the king outside the place where the fire had been lit. And the wizards said to their people: 'We shall not rise to our feet at his approach; for whoever rises at his approach

will believe in him afterwards and do obeisance to him.' Finally
St. Patrick rose and seeing their many chariots and horses, he came
to them, rather appropriately singing with heart and voice this verse
of the psalmist: 'Some may go in chariots and some on horses, but
we shall walk in the name of our God.' (*Psalms 19.8*). They did not
rise at his approach; but just one, with God's aid, refused to obey the
wizard's words, namely Ercc, son of Daeg, whose relics are now venerated in the city called Slane, and he rose; and Patrick blessed him, and
he believed in the eternal God.

They then began to talk with one another, and one of the two
wizards, called Lochru, was insolent to the saint's face and had the
effrontery to disparage the catholic faith in the most arrogant terms.
St. Patrick glared fiercely at him as he spoke, as once Peter did with
Simon, and then, with strange power, he shouted aloud and confidently addressed the Lord: 'O Lord, who can do all things and in
whose power all things lie, who sent me here, may this impious man
who blasphemes Your name be now carried up out of here and die
without delay.' At these words the wizard was carried up into the air
and then dropped outside from above; he fell head-first and crashed his
skull against a stone, was smashed to pieces and died before their eyes;
and the heathen were afraid.

18.   The king with his followers was angry with Patrick at this, and he
determined to kill him and said: 'Lay hands on this fellow who is
destroying us.' Then seeing that the ungodly heathen were about to
rush him, St. Patrick rose and said in a clear voice: 'May God arise and
His enemies be scattered and those who hate Him flee from His face.'
And immediately darkness fell on them, and there was a horrible sort
of upheaval and the ungodly attacked one another, one rising up against
the other; and there was a great earthquake which locked their chariot-
axles together and drove them off violently, and the chariots and horses
careered at break-neck speed over the flat plain, until in the end only a
few of them escaped half-dead to the mountain Monduirn. And this
blow laid low seven times seven men at Patrick's curse before the king
and his elders until the king was left with only seven others; there
were himself and his wife and two kings and another four followers.
And they were very frightened.

And the queen came to Patrick and said to him: 'Sir, you are just
and powerful; do not destroy the king; for the king will come and bow
the knee and worship your Lord.' And the king came, compelled by
fear, and bowed the knee before the saint and pretended to worship
Him whom he did not want to worship. And after they had taken leave
of each other, the king, going a little way off, called St. Patrick over
on some pretext, with the intention of killing him some way or other.
But Patrick, aware of the wicked king's thoughts, first blessed his

companions (eight men and a boy) in the name of Jesus Christ, and came to the king. The king counted them as they approached, and immediately they disappeared clean out of the king's sight; the heathen saw just eight deer with a fawn heading, as it were, for the wilds. And king Loegaire, saddened, frightened and humiliated, returned at dawn to Tara with the few survivors.

19   The following day, that is, Easter day, as the kings and princes and wizards were lying at ease at Loegaire's house (for that was their most important festival), as they ate and drank wine in Tara palace and some talked while others thought about what had happened, St. Patrick, accompanied by only five men, came to do battle and speak for the holy faith in Tara before all the peoples, though the doors were shut, just as we read about Christ.

     When he entered the banqueting-hall at Tara, not one of the number rose at his approach except one person only, Dubthach maccu Lugil, an excellent poet who had staying with him there at the time a certain young poet called Fiacc, who was afterwards an admirable bishop and whose relics are venerated at Sletty. As I said, this Dubthach was the only one of the heathen to rise in honour of St. Patrick; and the saint blessed him, and he was the first to believe in God that day, and it was counted to him as righteousness. And when they saw Patrick, he was invited by the heathen to eat his fill, so that they might test him about things to come. But he, knowing what was to come, did not refuse to eat.

20   Now while they were all feasting, that wizard Lucetmail, who had been involved in the clash during the night, was also provoked that day by his colleague's death to clash with St. Patrick; and to start off the contest, as the others looked on he poured something from his own goblet into Patrick's cup to test his reaction. And St. Patrick, seeing this kind of test, blessed his cup in the sight of all, and the liquid turned into something like ice; and when the cup was turned upside down only the drop which the wizard had poured in fell out. And he blessed the cup a second time; the liquid returned to its natural state, and everyone was amazed.

     After a little while the wizard said: 'Let us perform signs on this great plain.' And Patrick replied: 'What signs?' The wizard said: 'Let us bring snow upon the land.' And Patrick said: 'I refuse to bring what is contrary to God's will.' And the wizard said: 'I shall bring it in the sight of all.' Then he began his magical spells and brought snow upon the whole plain, deep enough to reach men's waists; and all saw and were amazed. And the saint said: 'Right, we can see this; now take it away.' He said: 'I cannot take it away before this time tomorrow.' And the saint said: 'You can do evil, and not good. It is not like that with me.' Then he gave his blessing over the whole plain round about, and the snow disappeared quick as a flash, without any rain, clouds or wind. And the crowds shouted and were quite amazed and were filled with remorse.

Soon after, the wizard invoked demons and brought very thick darkness on the land as a sign; and they all muttered. And the saint said: 'Drive away the darkness.' But he could not. And the saint gave a blessing in prayer, and suddenly the darkness was driven away and the sun shone. And they all shouted aloud and gave thanks. Now when all this had taken place between the wizard and Patrick before the king's eyes, the king said to them: 'Throw your books into water, and we shall venerate the one whose books come out unscathed.' Patrick replied: 'I shall do so.' And the wizard said: 'I refuse to undergo a trial by water with this man; for he considers water to be his god.' (No doubt he had heard of baptism performed with water by Patrick.) And the king replied: 'Then pass them through fire.' And Patrick said: 'I am ready.' But the wizard refused, saying: 'This man worships in turn in alternate years now water, now fire as his god.' And the saint said: 'Not so. But you go yourself, and one of my boys will go with you into a house which stands apart and is closed up, and my garment will be about you, and yours about my boy, and you will then be burned together.'

This plan was settled upon, and the house was built for them, with one half made of green wood and the other of dry wood. And the wizard was sent into the house, into the green part of it, with Patrick's robe round him, and one of St. Patrick's boys, called Benignus, with the magic cloak into the dry part of the house. And so the house was closed up on the outside and was set on fire before the whole crowd. And it came about in that hour, as Patrick prayed, that the fire's flames consumed the wizard with the green half of the house, leaving only St. Patrick's robe untouched - it was not touched by the fire. Benignus, on the other hand, was more fortunate, as was the dry half of the house; the fire did not touch him, as is written of the three boys, nor was he distressed nor did it inflict any harm, except that the wizard's robe which had been about him was burned up, by the will of God.

The king was very angry with Patrick over the wizard's death and almost rushed at him with the intention of killing him. But God prevented him. For at Patrick's prayer and at his voice the wrath of God came down on the ungodly people and many of them perished. And St. Patrick said to the king: 'Unless you believe now, you will very soon die; for God's wrath will come down upon your head.' And the king was terrified and shaken at heart, and the whole city with him.

21   So king Loegaire assembled the elders and all his council and said to them: 'It is better for me to believe than to die.' And after taking counsel,

on his followers'instructions he believed that day and turned to the
eternal Lord God, and many others believed there. And St. Patrick
said to the king: 'Because you opposed my teaching and were a
stumbling-block to me, though the days of your reign be prolonged,
no one of your seed shall be king after you for ever.'

22   And St. Patrick, according to the Lord Jesus' command going and
teaching all nations and baptising them in the name of the Father and
of the Son and of the Holy Ghost, set out from Tara and preached, with
the Lord working with him and confirming his words with the following
signs.

The Brussels and Vienna MSS (B and C) begin book 2 after this point.

23   There was in Patrick's day a man in the country of the Ulaid called
Macuil Maccugreccae, and this man was very ungodly, a cruel tyrant,
with the result that he was called 'Cyclops'. He was evil in thought, im-
moderate in word, malevolent in deed, bitter in spirit, irate in temper,
vicious in body, savage in mind, pagan in way of life, a monster in
conscience; he plumbed such depths of ungodliness that one day as
he sat in a rugged spot high up on the hills, called *Druim Mocceuchach*,
where he played the tyrant every day, displaying the most heinous
signs of savagery and killing passing strangers with criminal brutality,
he saw St. Patrick, radiant with the bright light of faith and resplendent
with some wondrous diadem of heavenly glory, walking on his leisurely
way with unshakeable confidence in his doctrine, and he decided to
kill him too, saying to his followers: 'Look, here comes that deceiver
and corruptor of men who is in the habit of performing his tricks to
deceive men and mislead many. So let us go and test him, and we shall
find out whether that God in whom he boasts has any power.'
    And they tested the holy man in this way; they put in their midst
one of their number, who was perfectly well, lying with a blanket over
him and pretending to be mortally ill, to put the saint to the test in
such a deception, calling the saint a deceiver, his miracles tricks and his
prayers sorcery and spells. When St. Patrick approached with his disciples,
the heathen said to him: 'Look, one of us has been taken ill now; so come
and chant some of your religion's spells over him, in the hope that he
may be healed.' Now St. Patrick, knowing all their wiles and deceptions,
said firmly and fearlessly: 'No wonder he was taken ill.' His companions
uncovered the face of the man pretending to be ill and saw that he was

already dead. They were dumbfounded and astonished at such a miracle and said mournfully to one another: 'Truly this is a man of God; we did wrong to test him.'

St. Patrick turned to Macuil and said: 'Why did you want to test me?' And the cruel tyrant replied: 'I regret doing it; I shall do whatever you tell me and I surrender myself into the power of your most high God whom you preach.' And St. Patrick said: 'Then believe in my God the Lord Jesus Christ and confess your sins and be baptised in the name of the Father and of the Son and of the Holy Ghost.' And he was converted in that hour and believed in God eternal, and was baptised. And then Macuil went on to say: 'I confess to you, my holy lord Patrick, that I intended to kill you; so judge what punishment is due for such a horrible crime.'

And Patrick said: 'I cannot judge, but God will judge. But as for you, go away unarmed to the sea and cross quickly from this land of Ireland, taking nothing of your possessions with you except some poor little garment with which to cover your body, and tasting nothing and eating nothing of the produce of this island, and with the mark of your sin on your head; and when you reach the sea, shackle your feet together with iron fetters and throw the key into the sea, and put yourself into a boat made of one skin, without rudder and without oar, and be ready to go wherever wind and sea may take you; and whatever land Divine Providence may bring you to, dwell in it and carry out God's command-ments there.' And Macuil said: 'I shall do as you say. But what shall we do about the dead man?' And Patrick said: 'He will live and get up without any pain.' And Patrick raised him in that hour, and he came back to life and health.

And Macuil journeyed from there as quickly as he could to the sea to the south of Magh Inis, in the unshakeable confidence of faith; he shackled himself on the shore, throwing the key into the sea as he had been instructed, and put out to sea in a boat. And a north wind blew on him and carried him southwards and cast him up on an island called *Evonia* (The Isle of Man). And he found there two most admirable men of shining faith and doctrine, who were the first to teach the Word of God and baptism in *Evonia*, and the islanders were converted by their teaching to the catholic faith; their names are Conindri and Rumili. Now when they saw the man with only one garment they were amazed and took pity on him and picked him up out of the sea, gladly welcoming him. So in the place where he had found spiritual fathers, in the land assigned to him by God, he trained body and soul in accordance with their rule and spent his whole lifetime with those two holy bishops until he was made their successor in the episcopate. This man is Macuil *dimane*, bishop and prelate of *Ardd Huimnonn*.

24   On another occasion, as St. Patrick was resting on the Lord's Day
on the sea-shore by the saltmarsh which is on the north side a short
distance away from Ox's Neck, he heard a noisy din coming from
pagans who were working on the Lord's Day making a rampart: so
Patrick called them over and forebade them to work on the Lord's
Day. But they did not comply with what the saint said; indeed they
laughed him to scorn. And St. Patrick said: 'Mudebrod, however much
you work, may it get you nowhere.' So it was fulfilled. For the following night a great wind arose and stirred up the sea, and the storm
destroyed all the pagans' work, in accordance with the saint's words.

25   There was in the country of Airthir a rich and respected man
called Daire. Patrick asked him to give him some place for his religious
observances. And the rich man said to the saint: 'What place do you
want?' 'I want,' said the saint, 'you to give me that piece of high ground
which is called Willow Ridge, and I shall build a place there.' But he
refused to give the saint that high ground, but gave him another site on
lower ground, where there is now the Martyrs' Graveyard near Armagh,
and St. Patrick lived there with his followers.
   But after some time there came a groom of Daire, bringing his remarkable horse to graze in the Christians' grassy meadow. And Patrick
was annoyed at the horse being brought in this way onto his ground and
said: 'Daire has acted stupidly in sending his brute beasts to disturb the
little ground that he gave to God.' But the groom like a deaf man did
not hear, and like a dumb man not opening his mouth he said nothing,
but let the horse loose there for the night and went away. But when the
groom came the following morning to see his horse, he found it already
dead. And returning home he sadly reported to his master: 'Look, that
Christian has killed your horse; the disturbance of his place annoyed him.'
And Daire said: 'Let him be killed too - go now and slay him.'
   But as they went outside death fell on Daire quick as a flash. And
his wife said: 'This death is because of the Christian. Someone go
quickly and have his blessings brought back to us, and you will be saved;
and let those who have gone off to kill him be stopped and recalled.'
Two men went off to the Christian, and concealing what had actually
happened said to him: 'Look, Daire has been taken ill; let something be
brought to him from you, in the hope that he may be cured.' And
St. Patrick, knowing what had happened, said: 'To be sure.' And he
blessed some water and gave them it, saying: 'Go, sprinkle your horse
with this water and take it with you.' And they did so, and the horse
came back to life; and they took it with them, and Daire was cured by
the sprinkling of the holy water.
   Afterwards Daire came to do honour to St. Patrick, bringing with him a
wonderful bronze bowl from across the sea, which could hold three metretae.

And Daire said to the saint: 'Look, take this bowl:' and Patrick said: *'Grazacham'*. And Daire returned home and said: 'He is a fool who says nothing better than *Grazacham* for a wonderful three *metretae* bowl.' and to his servants he added: 'Go and bring us back our bowl.' They went off and said to Patrick: 'We shall take the bowl.' And yet that time too St. Patrick said: *'Grazacham*, take it:' and they took it. And Daire asked his servants: 'What did the Christian say when you took the bowl back?' They replied: 'He said *Grazacham* again.' Daire replied: *'Grazacham* when you give it, *Grazacham* when you take it away: what he says is so good - his bowl will be brought back to him with these *Grazachams'*. And this time Daire came personally and brought the bowl back to Patrick, saying to him: 'Here, keep your bowl. For you are a firm, steadfast man. What is more, I give you, as far as it is mine to give, that piece of ground which you once requested, and live there.' And that is the city which is now called Armagh.

And they both went out, St. Patrick and Daire, to look at the wonderful offering and pleasing gift, and they climbed up to that high ground and found a hind with her little fawn lying on the spot where now there is the altar of the North church in Armagh. And Patrick's companions wanted to take hold of the fawn and kill it, but the saint refused and did not allow it; indeed the saint himself took the fawn, carrying it on his shoulders; and the hind followed him like a very gentle, docile ewe, till he had let the fawn go free in another wood lying to the north side of Armagh, where the knowledgeable say there are some signs remaining to this day of his miraculous power.

26 The knowledgeable tell of how a very hard and miserly man living in Magh Inis reached such a criminal degree of stupidity and greed that one day the fool forcibly drove away before St. Patrick's eyes, violently and irresponsibly, the two oxen which drew Patrick's cart, while the oxen were resting and grazing in his holding's pasture after their holy work. And St. Patrick was angry with him and said with a curse: *'Mudebrod*, you have done wrong. May neither you nor your descendants for ever have any benefit from this field; from now on it will be useless.' And so it came about. For a sea-flood came in that day, great enough to inundate and cover the whole field, and, as the prophet says, 'fertile land was turned into a salt-marsh because of the wickedness of the man who lived on it.' (*Psalm 106.34*) This land has been sandy and infertile from the day that St. Patrick cursed it right to the present day.

27 [And so, the Lord willing, I shall attempt to tell a few of the numerous miracles of Patrick.] Once, when the whole of Britain was frozen in the chill of unbelief, a certain king's remarkable daughter, called Monesan, full of the help of the Holy Spirit, when someone asked for her

hand in marriage, did not consent; nor could she be forced to what she did not wish and what was a worse course, even when she had large quantities of water poured over her. For amid beatings and drenchings with water she used to ask her mother and her nurse whether they knew the maker of the disc by which all the world is given light, and when she received an answer which gave her to know that the sun's maker is He whose seat is heaven, when she was repeatedly pressed to be united to a husband in the marriage bond, she would reply, enlightened by the brightly shining counsel of the Holy Spirit: 'I shall certainly not do this.' For she looked for the maker of all creation through nature, following in this the example of the patriarch Abraham.

Her parents embarked on a plan given them by God; they had heard that a man Patrick was visited by the eternal God every seventh day, and so they travelled over to Ireland with their daughter and appealed to Patrick, whom they found after a laborious search. Patrick proceeded to ask these newcomers questions; then the travellers began to cry out and say: 'It is because of our daughter's ardent desire to see God that we have been induced and compelled to come to you.' Then Patrick, filled with the Holy Spirit, raised his voice and said to her: 'Well, do you believe in God?' She replied: 'I do.' Then he bathed her in the holy baptism of water and the Spirit. Very soon after she fell prostrate on the ground and delivered up her spirit into the angels' hands. She was buried at the spot where she died. Then Patrick prophesied that after twenty years her body would be removed with all honour from there to a neighbouring cell - as in fact happened later. And the relics of this woman from across the sea are venerated to this day.

28   I shall give a brief account of a miracle amazingly worked by the apostolic and Christ-like Patrick, our present subject; it is written that it happened almost uniquely to him when he was still in the flesh and to Stephen. One time when he was going off through the darkness to his usual spot to pray, he saw the usual heavenly signs: and wishing to test his very dear, loyal and holy boy, he said: 'My son, tell me, please, whether you perceive what I do.' Then the young lad, called Benignus, said without hesitation: 'Now I realise what you perceive; for I see the heavens open and the Son of God and His angels.' Then Patrick said: 'Now I perceive that you are my worthy successor.' And without delay they hurried on and came to the usual spot for prayer. And as they prayed in the middle of the river-bed, the lad said: 'I cannot endure the coldness of the water any longer;' for the water was too cold for him. Then Patrick told him to step down from the higher to a lower position; but he could not stand there for long either, for he protested that he felt the water hot; then, unable to bear standing there for any length of time, he clambered onto the bank.

29   I shall not pass over in silence an amazing feat of Patrick. News came to him of the quite iniquitous action of a certain British king called Coroticus, an ill-starred and cruel tyrant. He was a very great persecutor and murderer of Christians. Now Patrick tried to recall him to the way of truth by means of a letter; but he scoffed at its salutary warnings. When this was reported to Patrick, he prayed to the Lord and said: 'God, if it be possible, cast this traitor out from this present world and the world to come.' After only a short time had elapsed, Coroticus heard someone give a musical performance and sing that he would soon pass from his royal throne; and all his dearest friends took up the cry. Then, when he was in open court, he suddenly had the misfortune to take on the appearance of a little fox; he made off before his followers' eyes, and from that day and that hour, like a passing stream of water, he was never seen anywhere again.

INDEX OF PROPER NAMES

(References are to chapter numbers. C=Confessio; E=Epistola; D=Dicta; M=Muirchu)

Abraham	C 39; E 18; M 27
Aegiptus	M 13
Aidus (Aed)	M pref.
Ail	M pref.
Airthir: see Orientales	
Alpes	M 6
Alsiodorum	M 6
Amat(h)or(ex)	M pref., 9
Ardd Huimnonn	M 23
Arddmach(a)e (Armagh)	M pref., 25
Augustinus	M 9
Auxerre: see Alsiodorum	
Auxilius	M 9
Babylon	M 15
Bannavem Taberniae	C 1; M 1
Benedictus	M 9
Benignus, Benineus, Bineus	M 20, 28
Boyne: see Colpdi	
Brega	M 11, 14
Brene	M 11
Britannia	M 27
Britanniae	C 23, 32, 43; M 1, 9
Britannicus	M 6, 29
Brito	M 1, 8
Caelestinus	M 8
Calpornius, Cualfarnius	C 1; M 1
Campus Inis(s)	M 12, 14, 23, 26
Cog(u)itosus	M pref.
Collum Bovis	M 24
Colpdi: see Hostium Colpdi	
Conalnei (Conaille)	M 11
Concessa	M 1
Conindri	M 23
Coolenni (Cualann)	M 11
Coroticus, Corictic, Coirthech	E 2, 6, 12, 19, 21; M pref., 29
Cruidneni (Cruithne)	M 11
Daeg	M pref., 17

Daire	M pref., 25
Dee: see Hostium Dee	
Dichu	M 11, 12, 14
Dorsum Salicis	M 25
Drogheda: see Hostium Colpdi	
Druim Moccuechach	M 23
Dubthach maccu Lugir	M pref., 19
Ebmoria	M 9
Ercc	M pref., 17
Eva	E 13
Evonia	M 23
Feecol Ferchertni	M 14
Fertae Martyrum	M 25
Ferti virorum Feec	M 14, 16
Fiacc	M 14, 16, 19
Foclut, Foclita	C 23; M 7
Franci	E 14
Galli	E 14
Galliae	C 43; D 1; M pref., 6
Gamaliel	M 6
Genesseon (Goshen)	M 13
Germanus	M pref., 6, 8
Helias	C 20: M 2
(H)erodis	M 16
Hiberionaces,-i	C 23; E 16
Hiberione	C 1, 16, 23, 28, 41, 62; E 1, 5, 10, 12
Hibernensis	M 23
Hibernia	M 27
Hibernicus	M 7
Hibernus	C 37
(H)orreum Patricii	M 11
Hostium Colpdi	M 14
Hostium Dee	M 11
Iacob	C 39; E 18
Inis: see Campus Inis	
Inverdee: see Hostium Dee	
Iohannes	M 2
Ionas	M 2
Isaac	C 39; E 18
Iserninus	M 9
Italia	D 1
Iudei	M 2
Lochru	M 10, 16, 17
Loiguire, Loegaire	M pref., 10, 15, 16, 18, 19, 21

Lothroch	M 10
Lucetmael, Lucetmail	M 10, 16, 20
Ma(c)cuil maccu Greccae	M pref., 23
Magh Inis: see Campus Inis	
Man, Isle of: see Evonia	
Melchisedec	M 9
Miliucc	M pref., 11, 12
Miss	M 11, 12
Monduirn	M 18
Mone(i)san	M pref., 27
Moysicus	M 2
Muirchu maccu Machtheni	M pref.
Nabcodonossor	M 15
Neill (Niall)	M 10
Orientales	M 25
Osee	C 40
Palladius	M pref., 8, 9
Paulus	M 6
Petrus	M 8, 17
Picti	E 2, 12, 15
Potitus	C 1; M 1
Roma	M 8
Romani	E 2, 12; D 3
Ronal	M 10
Rumili	M 23
Saul: see Horreum Patricii	
Saxonissa	M pref.
Scoticus	M 27
Scottus	C 41, 42; E 2, 12; D 3; M 10
Segitius	M 8
Simon	M 17
Slain (river Slane)	M 11
Slane	M 17
Slane: see Ferti virorum Feec	
Sleibti (Sletty)	M pref., 19
Slemish, Mt.: see Miss	
Sochet	M 1
Stephanus	M 28
Strangford Lough: see Brene	
Temoria (Tara)	M pref., 10, 15, 16, 18, 19, 22
Terrenum (mare)	D 1
Ulathi, Ulothi (Ulaid)	M 11, 12, 23
Ventre	M 1
Victoricus	C 23; M 1, 7, 11